A Funny Thing Happened On My Way To Work... I Retired

A Guide From Work To Life!

By
STEVE KIEFER

Tate Publishing, LLC

"A Funny Thing Happened on My Way to Work . . . I Retired"
by Steve Kiefer

Copyright © 2005 by Steve Kiefer. All rights reserved.

Published in the United States of America
by Tate Publishing, LLC
127 East Trade Center Terrace
Mustang, OK 73064
(888) 361-9473

Book design copyright © 2005 by Tate Publishing, LLC. All rights reserved.

No part of this publication may be reproduced, stored in a retrieval system or transmitted in any way by any means, electronic, mechanical, photocopy, recording or otherwise without the prior permission of the author except as provided by USA copyright law.

This book is designed to provide accurate and authoritative information with regard to the subject matter covered. This information is given with the understanding that neither the author nor Tate Publishing, LLC is engaged in rendering legal, professional advice. Since the details of your situation are fact dependent, you should additionally seek the services of a competent professional.

ISBN: 1-9331486-2-4

A tourist paused for a rest in a small town in the mountains. He went over to an old man sitting on a bench in front of the only store in town and inquired,

"Friend, can you tell me something this town is noted for?"

"Well," replied the old man, "I don't rightly know, except that it's the starting point to the world. You can start here and go anywhere you want."

Your retirement is your ticket to the world. Let's get going.

-Steve Kiefer

DEDICATION

I would like to dedicate this book to my lovely wife, Alice, who gave me the encouragement I needed to finish the project.

I also want to thank my daughter Brittney and my son Brandon for allowing me the time between ballgames to do the research.

I would also like to say a special thanks to John Fox who gave me the idea to right a book in the first place.

TABLE OF CONTENTS

Foreword 9
Introduction 11

Chapter One: Getting Our Sea Legs 19
Chapter Two: Twelve Steps to Atlantis 45
Chapter Three: Let's Start Building the Ship. 79
Chapter Four: What Makes You Seasick
      (Risk Tolerance). 109
Chapter Five: What is your "Net" Worth?. 139
Chapter Six: Nine Torpedoes that can Sink Your Ship
      And How to Avoid Them. 151
Chapter Seven: An Unexpected Iceberg
      Not Withdrawing Enough .167
Chapter Eight: Finding the "SS"
      (Social Security) Minnow 181
Chapter Nine: Picking the Right Captain. 207
Chapter Ten: Returning to the Crow's Nest. 221
Chapter Eleven: Captain's Log 239
Chapter Twelve: Docking Our Ship. 251

Summary 257
Appendix: Helpful Websites and Definitions. 259

FOREWORD

As a published author and a marketing coach in the financial services arena, it is my privilege to write this forward to Steve's book, *A Funny Thing Happened on my Way to Work - I Retired!*

The genesis for this book came as the distillation of many months of our working together. Steve's expertise, combined with his passion, all coalesced - distilled - into his book. And the lesson? If you work, you will retire. That is as certain as death and taxes. So, Steve shows, with wit and candor, proven ways to keep your retirement ship sailing safely from port to port; as opposed to sinking at the dock through lack of foresight and maintenance.

Steve also weaves an ethical vision throughout the book. For he lived his book as a child. His dream - his passion - has been helping thousands of people, just like you, build their ship of dreams. And he lives what he preaches - what a refreshing rarity in today's cynical world.

A Funny Thing Happened on my Way to Work - I Retired! is not a textbook. It is written for the average person, you and me, who need practical advice for preparing for the future. So please read it. But, also do what Steve recommends.

Your ship has already come in. It is up to you to steer it the right way.

John Fox
Author and Business Coach
fox@cedevices.com
Salt Lake City, Utah

INTRODUCTION

The old saying goes, "There are no atheists in foxholes." The same may be said of a ship in a storm. It is interesting that when a ship hits rough seas and starts rolling in a heavy gale, her passengers begin to think about their past sins and shortcomings in life. Contrast that to a heavy fog where the same ship is slowly groping her way through the thick mist, the passengers will go to bed and sleep soundly. Yet, they are in the greatest danger at sea in a fog. It has been the cause of more disasters than all the storms that ever blew.

On Sunday night, April 14, 1912, the people on the Titanic were oblivious to the danger that they were in. That evening the air was bitterly cold, the sea unusually *still*. On the bridge, the captain and his officers discussed how difficult it was to see icebergs on calm, clear, moonless nights because there was no wind to kick up white surf around the iceberg and there was only starlight by which to see.

Before going to bed, the captain ordered the lookouts to keep a sharp watch for ice. At 11:40 P.M., high up in the crow's nest on the forward mast, the lookout peered out into the darkness. He didn't have binoculars. They were misplaced before the ship left Southampton.

Suddenly, he saw something: a huge, dark, looming shape directly in the ship's path, about 500 yards ahead (or about thirty-seven seconds ahead). He quickly sounded the alarm, but it was not timely. The ship did avoid striking the iceberg head-on. (Some think a head-on collision might have caused less damage to the hull).

Rather, the ice dealt the Titanic a glancing blow, rupturing the hull intermittently along her starboard side. The ship had entered an ice field that was seventy-eight miles long. It only

A Funny Thing Happened on My Way to Work . . . I Retired

took about twenty minutes for those in charge to realize that the ship was about to sink. The unthinkable would be its destiny. The Titanic was going down.

In the coming pages, I will show you how to calm the seas of retirement and how to avoid the "icebergs" that will inevitably get in your way. Together, we will build a sea-worthy vessel to endure the storms that will come. And they *will* come. And somewhere in the process we will find a point of reference to work from. (More on this later). We have a lot of work to do in the coming pages, but don't worry; I'll give you plenty of recesses to help you cope with the exertion. Speaking of recess, as you progress through the exercises in this book, you'll begin to feel like you're back in school. As a result, you'll be tempted to come up with excuses to get out of this exercise or that exercise. Don't do it! Someone once said that excuses are "the skin of reason stuffed full of lies." You *can* make excuses all day long but there will always be one person you can never fool . . . YOU.

The Toronto Star invited teachers to submit excuses they had received from their students. They received these examples:

- A student explaining why he was late: "I was kidnapped by aliens and interrogated for three hours."
- Another student, telling why he had failed to turn in his essay: "The bus driver read it and liked it so much he kept it to show to his passengers."
- Another: "I got mugged on the way to school. I offered him my money, my watch, and my penknife—but all he wanted was my essay."
- Mike, a 14-year-old, came up with a "watertight" excuse for arriving at school an hour late with his pants soaked to the knees: "I was just about to board the bus when I found I'd lost my ticket. Since it would take too long to walk to school, I hopped a fence onto a golf course.

I headed for a creek that crisscrossed several fairways until I found a likely spot for lost balls. Retrieving three balls from their watery graves, I then made for the clubhouse where I sold the balls for bus fare. And that's why I'm late."

Even adults get into the game of making excuses. Following are some actual notes that were sent to school with the student. (The names are changed).

- "Please excuse Mary for being absent yesterday. She was bothered by very close veins."
- "Fred has an acre in his side."
- My son is under the doctor's care and should not take P.E. today, "one parent wrote. "Please execute him."
- "My daughter is **not** illiterate. Her father and I were married before she was born!"
- "Please excuse Billy for being absent. He was sick and I had him shot."
- "Please excuse Sam for being . . . It was his father's fault."

Resist the temptation to make excuses for cutting corners in the coming chapters. Yes, some of the work will be challenging, but it WILL be worth it.

You'll find in the coming pages that I love using illustrations. They are fun, interesting and they help me paint a vivid picture of the point I am trying to make. I have learned through my years of public speaking that illustrations can dramatically raise the level of retention and make the journey more palatable.

Let's begin our journey by discussing the topic of *setting goals*. As some wise person once said, "If we don't know where we are going, how will we know when we get there?"

When I was ten years old, my parents decided to get

A Funny Thing Happened on My Way to Work . . . I Retired

a divorce. My mother packed five siblings and a dog into the family's '66 Bonneville Pontiac and moved us from a beautiful 70-acre farm in Indiana. We landed in an old rent house in a dusty little town somewhere in New Mexico. I was 1,500 miles away from my home. For the next eight years I dreamed of going back to that farm and getting away from the so-called "Land of Enchantment" that never enchanted me. The day following my High School graduation, I was on a bus heading east. I made a quick stop in Oklahoma to visit some close friends. I planned to continue my journey back to my roots. *Three years* later, I traveled from there to Arkansas to work as a counselor at Lake Nixon Day Camp for the summer. That was 25 years ago . . . I never made it back to Indiana.

Do I have regrets? Let's see. I have a wonderful wife, and two of the most precious children in the world. I am a leader in my community and church and have established a strong investment business in Little Rock.

"Yes, but do you have regrets?" Let's put it this way, if I could take everything I have now and move it to a farm . . . I would. But I have no regrets.

"What does that have to do with retirement?" you say. The answer is simple: *Goals are put in place to be aimed at but they are not always hit, AND THAT'S OKAY!* Getting close to the goal is sometimes better than hitting it dead center.

A young man was riding his bicycle across campus at a university. Someone sitting on the bench noticed a message on the cyclist's shirt announcing his goal in life. The message read, "I'm going to be a doctor." When the young man rode by, the observer noticed a small license plate on the bicycle that read, "I'm going to be a Mercedes." The issue is not what you are today, the issue is what your goals can help you become tomorrow. Retirement is a goal we want to achieve and so we take careful aim at the prize. But, economic currents and unexpected troubles cause our shot to veer off course and we miss the mark. Does that mean we have failed? Absolutely not, but, the more we intentionally manage those things we can control, the closer our shot will be to the bull's eye. That's what this book is all about—

Helping you aim for the center of your retirement goal and hitting it as close as you can.

We will explore psychological as well as practical approaches toward retirement that will equip you to handle just about any roadblock that you encounter during your retirement process. Soldiers are good examples of this process: They have offensive weapons like a rifle and hand-grenades, and they are equipped with defensive gear such as a flack-jacket and helmet. The offensive weapons give the soldier power to destroy threats before the enemy can inflict injury. The defensive equipment protects the life of the soldier and allows him to endure and survive an adversarial attack.

When you are finished with this book, you will have offensive weapons to neutralize many would-be threats to your retirement. You will also be equipped with methods that will help your retirement survive when unstoppable storms arrive.

People planning to retire are faced with a bewildering array of questions, tax rules, and investment possibilities. Just sorting out the potential financial options and obstacles can be an overwhelming task. That is precisely why the time to prepare for your retirement event is now.

Norman Lawson tells of two friends who were visiting over coffee. One of them was very harried–frazzled in fact. It was just a few days before Christmas, and she wasn't ready. She hadn't gotten the cards out; hadn't purchased any presents yet; didn't have a tree yet. In fact, the friend was complaining that Christmas was a terrible time because she was never ready! "But, my dear," her friend commented, "didn't you know it was coming?" We know to the day when Christmas will come for the next thousand years, but people still act as though it snuck

A Funny Thing Happened on My Way to Work . . . I Retired

up on them. **YOUR RETIREMENT IS COMING. ARE YOU READY?**

As you move through the upcoming chapters, keep one thing at the forefront of your mind: *Retirement is what you make it!* I can give you all of the necessary tools to build a profitable and rewarding retirement, but it will be up to you to make them work.

One of Robert Ripley's famous *BELIEVE IT OR NOT* cartoons pictured a plain bar of iron worth $5. This same bar of iron, when made into horseshoes, would be worth $10.50. If it were made into needles its worth would jump to $3,285. And, if it were turned into balance springs for fine watches, its worth would skyrocket to $250,000. The same is true of your retirement. It is raw material. This book will help you to turn your retirement into a valuable asset that can go on for generations, but it will be up to you to decide whether it will be horseshoes or watch springs.

(This book is intended for workers who are approaching retirement; however, the principles contained herein are applicable to anyone in the work force and beyond).

*Someone once said, "After a
person makes his mark
in the world,
a lot of people begin
showing up with erasers."*

-Anonymous

CHAPTER ONE

GETTING OUR SEA LEGS

In his exciting book, A STRATEGY FOR WINNING, (New York: The Lincoln-Bradley Publishing Group, 1991) Carl Mays tells the story of the late Dave Thomas. Thomas never knew where he was born. An orphan, he left his foster parents at a young age to make a name for himself in the world. He did it.

His first full-time job was as a busboy in a restaurant in Knoxville, Tennessee. He went on to work for Kentucky Fried Chicken under Colonel Harlen Sanders. (More about the Colonel later in the book). Known for his hard work and mental capacity, he was asked to go to Columbus, Ohio, and save four small restaurants that were failing.

With little trouble, Dave Thomas turned those stores around. With this success, he decided to take his profits and open up his own restaurant. We know his second success as Wendy's Restaurants, named after his daughter. The Wendy's chain consists of over 3,500 restaurants and is one of the top three fast-food eateries in the country. Dave Thomas was the proud winner of the Horatio Alger award for going from poverty to accomplishment. Dave Thomas, with his meek temperament, will be greatly missed.

For many, however, this is not the case. Countless hard-working Americans have tried to increase their quality of life, but have failed. They don't fail because they're lazy; they fail because they don't have a *plan* to follow.

I ran into this situation a great many times when I began working in the investment business. Back then I decided to build a prospect list by going door-to-door and introducing myself to

A Funny Thing Happened on My Way to Work . . . I Retired

anyone who was home. As you can imagine, I met all types of people. But the ones that still stick in my mind today are those who told me they were so poor from being on a fixed income they could barely afford to pay their bills, much less scrape enough money together to invest. These where hard working families that spent decades in the workplace, only to come away with a small pension (if they were one of the fortunate ones) and an even smaller Social Security check.

My heart goes out to people in this situation, but I am powerless to help them. What needs to be done must be done *before* retirement arrives. **That is why I believe in preempting your retirement plan!** It can help you avoid a life of anxiety and financial struggle that so many Americans needlessly endure today.

In this chapter, we will discuss:

- Current retirement trends
- A "nostalgic" history of the baby boomers (You'll like this)
- Conclusion

CURRENT RETIREMENT TRENDS

Before we delve into the subject of retirement, let's look at some sobering facts:

1. An estimated one third of retirement needs are covered by Social Security (about 38%). In order to live on Social Security without the aid of additional income, one would be required to drastically reduce their standard of living. (Much more on Social Security later).

2. In 1900, the average life expectancy was 47 years; in 1990, it increased to 75 years. If they keep this up, Methuselah, who, according to the Bible, was 969 years

old when he died, will look like a young man. Talk about outliving your money! (Just kidding).

3. Due to changes in the corporate climate and advances in medicine, people are retiring earlier and living longer.

4. Healthy people may expect to spend as much time in retirement as they spend working. At the writing of this book, my father-in-law, P. B. Wooldridge was 89 years old. He retired at age 65 from the Cotton Belt Railroad Company. He is 24 years into his retirement and showing no signs of slowing down.

5. For the first time in history there will be more seniors than teenagers. Before you break into a chorus of, "We have overcome," keep in mind that fewer teenagers mean fewer workers who will contribute to Social Security. (Again, more about this later).

6. Over 70 percent of the current working population has no estate of *any* significance other than life insurance. The majority of baby boomers haven't saved for retirement. Ben Stein, speaking before Congress said "More than 77 million baby boomers are approaching retirement who are seriously under-prepared and have underestimated the income needed to support their envisioned retirement lifestyle." I really hope you are not one of them because they are in for a long and rough ride. If you are, we have urgent work to do.

7. Few workers have estimated how much it will take to fund a comfortable retirement. According to the Employee Benefit Research Institute many workers have unrealistic expectations about how much of their pre-retirement income they will need when they retire. I've seen some

workers estimate that they can survive on about 40% of their current income. Maybe on the planet Nirvana but not on planet Earth! One thing worse than not setting goals is setting *unrealistic* goals–not just goals you can't hope to reach, but also goals you can't live up to.

There is a silly story going around that makes a powerful point about where many of us are right now with goal setting. According to the story, Pope John Paul II needed a heart transplant. There was much concern throughout the Roman Catholic world. Everyone gathered outside the Vatican screaming, and waving their hands. "Take my heart, Pope, take my heart!"

Well, the Pope was deeply moved but didn't know what to do. Then an idea popped into his head. He asked the crowd to be quiet for a few minutes as he explained to them what he planned to do. He decided to throw down a feather. Whoever the feather landed on, was the one the pope would use for his heart transplant. Pope John Paul II then threw the feather down upon the people. Everyone began screaming and waving their hands again, "Take my heart, Pope, take my heart" but with one minor difference: now they were leaning their heads back and blowing the feather away from them back into the air shouting. "Take my heart, Pope (blow), Take my heart (blow)."

If you have no intention of reaching a goal, don't waste your time setting it. New Year's resolutions are set with good intentions but usually result in more guilt because of failure. And remember, "The road to Hell is paved with good intentions." Keep it real.

8. Upcoming retirees have given little or no thought to the managing of their funds *after* the retirement event: On July 20th, 1969 NASA landed two men on the moon. Four days later they landed those men back on Earth. The

retirement planning journey has some similarities. It also has two phases; the first phase is to accumulate capital and the second is to provide a lifetime of income. Like the moon mission, the second phase of retirement planning is much different than the first. This phase is more challenging, critically important, and has less room for error. Yet the first phase tends to attract the most attention.

Focusing on the management of your retirement money is as important as saving it. There is so much more to retirement income than simply liquidating a few shares of a fund to live on. When you make it to retirement, your journey is *half* over. You've had to survive market volatility, income changes, tax issues and more. Guess what? As a retiree you will have to survive market volatility, income changes, tax issues and more. (I sound like a broken record don't I?)

The point I'm trying to make is that I want you to be warned about letting your guard down when you achieve retirement. Don't wait until the day you get your gold watch to begin thinking about changing your source of income.

During the winter of 1979–80, I was visiting my friend Robert Cast in Atoka, Oklahoma. The previous night brought a huge ice storm that had settled on the area. The next morning Robert and I awoke to a world of shining glass. It just so happened that Robert's house was on a steep hill in town. I could see the sidewalk covered in glimmering enticement, and, being the brilliant college student that I was, I suggested that Robert and I build a makeshift sled and test the laws of physics.

We found an old piece of masonite siding and got into position. The sidewalk stretched for two full blocks before leveling off. We were off! (No pun intended). About halfway down, with tears in our eyes from laughter and freezing wind, it dawned on me . . . how are we going to stop? We were going too fast to jump off and besides; the trip was already over. Before I knew it we were airborne. The sidewalk had ended and so did the smooth ride.

Cars had been driving on the slippery roads and had worn grooves in the ice. My "derriere" hit a rut and stopped me instantly. (I lost two inches of height that day). I couldn't even cough without pain shooting up from my backside. Robert sailed over me and rolled to a stop at the base of a huge oak. We still talk about the "ice storm" to this day (with moaning) and we will never forget the cost of poor planning.

a. 66% of workers have given little or no thought to how they will *manage* their retirement dollars to insure they will not outlive their income.
b. 70% have given little or no thought about how they will *fund health expenses* that are not fully covered by Medicare, such as deductibles, long-term care, and prescription drugs.
c. 79% of workers have given little or no thought concerning how *to pay for long-term* care in the event of an extended stay at a nursing home or when long and costly home health care is required.

This lack of forethought reminds me of the Leaning Tower of Pisa. It has not always been called the Leaning Tower of Pisa. Built from 1173 to 1372, the twelve-story, solid marble structure stands 17 feet out of line. After the first three stories were completed, the ground underneath began to sink. I don't know about you, but if a foundation that I was working on began to sink after only three floors were finished, I DON'T THINK I WOULD BUILD NINE MORE STORIES ON TOP OF IT! But the builders didn't see it that way and thus it continues to lean farther and farther until someday it will topple.

Failing to plan for post-retirement money management may not be a problem at first. But, in a few years it can begin to lean until the day comes when you hear a retiree's most dreaded phrase: "You've run out of money."

9. In 2004 only 24% of workers were very confident they would have enough money to live comfortably throughout their retirement years.
Below is a chart showing the results of a 2004 survey, which asked workers to express their level of confidence toward retirement subjects.

2004		
Subject of Worker Confidence	**Number of Workers Who Are:**	
	Very Confident	Not as Confident
I believe I will have enough money to take care of basic expenses	36%	64%
I believe I am doing a good job of preparing financially for retirement	26%	74%
I donít believe I will outlive my retirement savings because I will have good money management after retirement	23%	77%
I believe I will have enough money to take care of medical expenses	21%	79%
I believe I will having enough money to pay for long-term care out-of-pocket	16%	84%

10. In 1997, persons 65 and older numbered 34.1 million. By 2030 this number will grow somewhere between 70 and 76 million because of the "boomers" reaching retirement age.

In 1992 some strange events were occurring in Colorado prisons according to an issue of Life magazine that year. Prison officials where perplexed by the growing number of inmates who were choosing to serve out their whole prison sentences rather than bargain for less time at parole hearings.

Since Colorado's prisons were overcrowded, and since parole hearings often resulted in less time in jail, prison officials were dumbfounded by this new trend. Was it due to a guilty conscience? Was it a peak season for penance? Probably not. According to state prison director Frank Gunter, the depressed economy on the outside made life on the inside look more comfortable. Many of the prisoners foresaw living on the streets when they got out, so prison didn't look so bad to them during a recession.

Perhaps after reading the statistics above, coupled with other doubts produced by unsure economic trends, bad news on the television (is there any other kind?) and personal fears, you have decided that it would be better to *stay* in the workforce and avoid the "unknowns" of retirement. Maybe you think you aren't well prepared and would feel safer behind "bars." Whoa! Slow down there partner! As someone once said, "give hope a chance." Many of those "unknowns" you are thinking about will be answered in the coming pages and those that aren't answered immediately will be discovered by following the guidelines provided. Don't stay in prison out of fear.

Keep in mind that the statistics mentioned above are based on a worker's personal confidence in his or her level of knowledge regarding retirement. Nothing raises confidence like knowledge and nothing lowers it like doubt.

A construction crew was laying a drain line as part of a new building. While excavating, the workers uncovered a power cable directly in the path of their work. The excavation was halted. An electrician was called in. The electrician came and looked at the cable. He assured workers that the cable was dead. "Go ahead and cut it out of the way," the electrician told the workers. The foreman asked, "Are you sure there is no danger?" "Absolutely," was the reply. Then the foreman asked, "Well, then, will you cut it for us?" The electrician hesitated for a moment, and then answered, "I'm not *that* sure." (Robert H. Spain, How to stay alive as long as you live Nashville: Dimensions for Living, 1992, p. 136)

That's putting your money where your mouth is! Doubt can lower your confidence but knowledge can raise it significantly.

I remember going to the 'ol swimming hole with a couple of my friends back on the farm when I was about nine. It had been a while since anyone had swam there. It was too scary for me to be the first one to jump in. What if there were snakes in the water? What if there was a giant snapping turtle? What if there was a fresh-water shark that escaped from a mutation lab and . . . SPLASH! My best friend just jumped in. I couldn't believe it, he just jumped . . . SPLASH! The other friend jumped in and both were having a blast. Suddenly I found myself sailing through the air . . . SPLASH! *I* hit the water in perfect cannon ball form. What changed my mind?

KNOWLEDGE!

Seeing my friends jump into the water and come back up to the surface unharmed told my brain that my fears were unfounded. I *knew* it was safe to go into the water. Give this book a chance. It will give you the knowledge you need to raise your confident level enough for you to . . . SPLASH!

Now, about those baby boomers:

WHO THE "BOOMERS" ARE AND HOW MANY

What is it about these strange creatures referred to as "baby boomers" we keep hearing about? (Ok, I confess. I am one myself.) Gone are the days of fat company pension plans, and rock solid Social Security confidence. At the end of WWII, there were 42 workers paying into Social Security for each person receiving benefits. Today, barely three people contribute for each recipient. Projections are, that by 2030, when most baby boomers will have retired, just two working people will contribute for each person receiving benefits.

According to the AARP there are 76 million baby boomers beginning to retire in droves. In fact one boomer reaches age fifty every 7.5 seconds! Most will retire within five years. Because boomers are chronologically, physically and psychologically younger than their parents were when they retired, retirement will be very different for them, us–you.

Baby boomers are becoming aware that they are experiencing a different type of retirement than the previous generation.

Compared to other generations, these confident and independent baby boomers willingly admit that:

- They need more money than their parents' generation to live comfortably. Inflation has left wrinkles on the face of retirement.
- Their generation is more self-indulgent than their parents.' They are higher consumers of merchandise than their predecessors.
- They will be healthier and expect to live longer.

Most baby boomers (that group of us born between 1946 and 1964) believe they will still be working during their retirement years. Eight in ten say they plan to work at least part-time and others envision starting their own business or working full-time according to an AARP Segmentation Analysis: Baby Boomers Envision Their Retirement.

68% of workers say they plan to work for pay during retirement. The reasons for work vary:

a. **Keeping health insurance or other health benefits. (43%)**
b. **Earning extra money to make ends meet. (36%)**
c. **Earning money to buy extra things. (36%)**
d. **Being able to support children or other relatives. (21%)**
e. **Because work is enjoyable and they want to stay involved. (64%)**
f. **Finally, to try a different career. (16%)**

As I mentioned above, 68% plan to work during retirement, but the reality is only one third (32%) of all retirees have reported actually going back to work for pay during retirement. (Employee Benefit Research Institute).

If you are one of the few who don't plan to work for pay after retirement, this section of the book is moot. However, if you are in the majority and plan to seek some type of employment, please read on:

*A **very** important word of caution here; planning to work after retirement implies two very **large** assumptions:*

1. You will be healthy enough to work at the *kind* of job you want to, **and** you will have enough stamina to work *long* hours if the job requires it.

2. There will be an attractive job available for you *when* you desire to be employed. Many greeting and burger flipping jobs are out there but do you want to work for minimum wage? I'm not saying there is anything wrong with this type of employment but realistically, did you work 30 or 40 years so you could end up greeting grouchy people at the front of the store?

As you can see, working for pay after retirement is not actually attempted by many retirees (only 32%), but more importantly, knowing *why* a retiree would want or need to work during retirement is crucial. If it is because you want to earn money to buy extra things, or because work is simply enjoyable, or because you want to try a different career, I see no reason not to plan for and expect to work during your retirement years.

However, if you plan to seek employment after retirement because you need to use the wages to keep your health insurance current, or you need the extra money just to make ends meet, or, because you will have to support a loved one, you'd better think again. I'm not saying you shouldn't plan to work for these reasons, but you must realize that your risk is elevated when you *have* to work after retirement as apposed to just *wanting* to work.

A LITTLE HISTORY

Let's take a quick look at some history and current trends of the boomers before we take a break. The official years of the baby boom generation (1946 through 1964) saw a marked increase in the number of births in North America. Here's how the birthrate rose and fell during the baby boom years:

1940 - 2,559,000 births per year

1946 - 3,311,000 births per year
1955 - 4,097,000 births per year — **Baby Boom**
1957 - 4,300,000 births per year
1964 - 4,027,000 births per year

1974 - 3,160,000 births per year

That's a bunch of babies! I'll bet the storks were ready to go on strike.

Steve Kiefer

CURRENT TRENDS

There are just a few more important statistics I want you to be aware of and then we can go to recess. Stay with me.

The fact is *older* boomers, those born between 1946 and 1955, had a median household net worth of just $146,050 in 2001, according to an analysis of Federal Reserve data by AARP. That may sound impressive, but consider the fact that half of this net worth was accounted for by savings accounts, mutual funds and other financial assets with the rest tied up in *home equity*. Ouch.

When we exclude home equity we find that a typical household in America has a net worth under $15,000. It is estimated that without Social Security almost one half of Americans over 65 would live *under* the poverty level. Can you believe this? Almost one out of every two Americans would exist under the poverty level were it not for Social Security. I DON'T want this to happen to you or your loved ones. It doesn't have to. (Remember the results of my door-knocking endeavor discussed earlier).

According to the Bureau of Labor Statistics, men retired at an average age of 62 between 1995 and 2000, and women quit at 61 1/2. In 1950, the average retirement age was 67. Be very careful about early retirement. Even when companies offer big severance packages, it is wise to run a full analysis of future income verses expenses to see if waiting a few more years would be financially beneficial. Although I won't be going into detail regarding the subject of early retirement here, I want to stress a couple of points:

1. Retiring before your scheduled age (see the chart in chapter eight to find this), can cost you a tremendous amount of income in the future from Social Security. In addition, most pensions begin compounding faster during a worker's latter years because of the larger amount

it has grown to. 8% of $10,000 is nothing compared to 8% of $500,000. ($800 verses $40,000).

2. The second point is related to the first. Workers tend to be in their best earning years just prior to retirement. Consider the following categories of earning potentials over the total career of an individual:
   a. The beginning investment years 18–30 years old
   b. The good investment years 31–45 years old
   c. The high-dollar investment years 46–65
   d. The retirement years 66–969 (Methuselah would be in this category)

As you can see from these investment categories, the best investment potential is between 46 and 65 years. The last five years of this category generally produce the highest earnings in one's career. If you are making $100,000 a year in income and you retire at the age of 62, you will forfeit $300,000 in wages, three years of pension contributions, compounding of your past contributions, AND you will have to take three years worth of income from your pension to live on. Depending on your current level of income, the losses can easily be in the tens of thousands of dollars. If you elect to draw Social Security at age 62, you will take a deduction in payout. Just how much of a deduction will be based on your birth date. (More on this in the "Social Security" chapter). Consider early retirement carefully before making any decisions.

Many seniors have been forced back to work. The impact of the new global economy and the financial effects of the lengthy bear market on 401(k) plans have affected thoughts of retirement. With little net worth to fund retirement, there is an exodus out of retirement back to the workforce. By 2015, estimates the National Council on the Aging, 20% of the U.S. work force will be over age 55, up from 13% in 2000. This brings home the point I was trying to make earlier. If you retire thinking you can always go back to work if things get tight, realize that the trend is already way ahead of you. People are finding it *necessary* to go back to work now and the indications are it's only going to get more crowded. Stay clear of that quicksand.

Let me reiterate; I'm not trying to scare you but I want you to be well informed regarding the trends you will be facing in retirement. After all, some surprises are unpleasant.

Back on our farm we had a big horse tank. Horse tanks were big oval shaped water troughs made out of concrete. Usually they were put in at ground level like a swimming pool but this one was on top of the ground sitting in the middle of our pasture.

I was sitting down playing in the tank one afternoon (when it was empty of course) and stood up for something. I noticed my little brother Kevin standing a few yards away. He had a look of terror on his face when he saw me and started sprinting toward the house. I was confused by his behavior for about one and a half seconds, then . . . **whack!** I saw a brilliant array of bright lights before I went to my knees. A rock had nailed me in the side of the head. It took me a few moments to realize what had happened. Apparently Kevin decided to throw a rock at the horse tank to see if he could make it in. According to him just when he released the salvo, I stood up. He knew immediately that the rock was going to bean me in the head so he did what all smart little brothers do when they know they're going to get pounded, he ran. That was an unpleasant surprise for both of us but mostly for me. I don't want *you* to get "whacked" with some unexpected problem that you weren't prepared for. (And no, I didn't beat him up but I sure told on him).

RECESS!

Let's get away from all of those depressing statistics for a moment and have some fun. Let's explore a bit of humorous history that most of our boomer companions can relate to.

A Funny Thing Happened on My Way to Work . . . I Retired

How do you know you're getting close to the blessed retirement event? Read on.

YOU KNOW YOU'RE GETTING CLOSE TO RETIREMENT WHEN:

- Your joints are more accurate than the National Weather Service.
- Your investment in health insurance is finally beginning to pay off.
- The twinkle in your eye is only the reflection of the sun on your bifocals.
- You finally got your head together, now your body is falling apart.
- You wake up with that morning-after feeling and you didn't do anything the night before.
- You don't care where your wife goes, just so you don't have to go along.
- It takes twice as long to do half as much.
- Many of your co-workers were born the same year that you got your last promotion.
- People call at 8 PM and ask, "Did I wake you?"
- Clothes you've put away until they come back in style . . . have come back in style.
- You look forward to a dull evening.
- Your mind makes contracts your body can't keep.
- The pharmacist has become your new best friend.
- There's nothing left to learn the hard way.
- You come to the conclusion that your worst enemy is gravity.
- You quit trying to hold your stomach in, no matter who walks into the room.
- Your idea of a night out is sitting on the patio.
- You look for your glasses for half-an-hour, and then find they've been on your head all the time.
- The only thing you exercise is caution.

- You wake up, looking like your driver's license picture.
- Happy hour is a nap.
- You begin every other sentence with, "Nowadays . . ."
- You don't remember when your wild oats turned to shredded wheat.
- You wonder how you could be over the hill when you don't remember being on top of it.
- Getting lucky means you find your car in the parking lot.
- The little gray-haired lady you help across the street is your wife.
- Your idea of weight lifting is standing up.
- It takes longer to rest than it did to get tired.
- The end of your tie doesn't come anywhere near the top of your pants.
- Your new easy chair has more options than your car.
- Your little black book only contains names ending in M.D.
- Everything hurts, and what doesn't hurt, doesn't work.
- You have too much room in the house and not enough in the medicine cabinet.
- Getting a little "action" means you don't need to take a laxative.
- Younger women start opening doors for *you*.
- Youthful injuries return with a vengeance.

I hope you enjoyed this little "exercise" in humor. If you can't or don't laugh at yourself I'm sure you can find someone who will.

A few years ago there was a report submitted to a State Industrial Commission regarding a man injured while in the act of repairing a chimney. He says, "When I got to the building, I found that the hurricane had knocked some bricks off the top. So I rigged up a beam with a pulley at the top of the building and hoisted up a couple of barrels full of bricks. When I had fixed the chimney, there were a lot of bricks left over. I hoisted the barrel back up again and secured the line at the bottom, and then went and filled the barrel with extra bricks. Then I went to the bottom and cast off the line.

"Unfortunately, the barrel of bricks was heavier than I was, and before I knew what was happening, the barrel started down, jerking me off the ground. I decided to hang on and halfway up I met the barrel coming down and received a severe blow on the shoulder. I then continued to the top, banging my head against the beam and getting my finger jammed in the pulley.

"When the barrel hit the ground, it burst its bottom, allowing the bricks to spill out. I was heavier than the empty barrel, and so I started down again at high speed. Halfway down, I met the barrel coming up and received a severe injury to my shins. When I hit the ground, I landed on the bricks, getting several painful cuts from the sharp edges. At this point I must have lost my presence of mind, because I let go of the line. The barrel then came down giving me another heavy blow on the head and putting me in the hospital . . ."

Sometimes we have to step back and laugh because it won't do any good to cry. Seriously, it is very healthy to find humor in life, even if life seems un-funny. If you are one who has trouble seeing the lighter side of life, maybe it's time for a change.

The year was 1934. A National Football League championship game was played between the New York Giants and the heavily favored Chicago Bears. The game was played in bitter cold weather, on a field covered with ice. At half time the Bears were leading 10–3.

During the half-time break, however, the Giants switched from cleats to sneakers, which they borrowed from the Manhattan College basketball team. Suddenly, the Giants had the edge. With their superior traction, they scored four touchdowns in the second half and beat the Bears 30–13.

If you are not able to beat the blues because your sense of humor is sense-less, change your shoes! Easier said than done? Maybe not.

David McClellan, a psychologist at Harvard University, once did a study that has some interesting implications. He had a group of students watch a film about Mother Teresa while he monitored their body's production of antibodies. Antibodies, of course, help us fight off infection. He discovered that as the students watched this uplifting film, their antibody level rose significantly; even for those who did not like Mother Teresa (some thought her a fraud). He then showed the students a film on Attila the Hun and their antibody levels dropped. The implication is clear. The things we focus on can affect the way we feel. If we want a feeling of well being in life, we have to focus on what's good in life.

Let's take another nostalgic look. This time take a walk with me down memory lane.

DO YOU REMEMBER . . . ?

Candy cigarettes
Wax coke-shaped bottles with colored sugar water inside
Soda pop machines that dispensed glass bottles
Hoola hoop contests
> (It's funny that my spell checker didn't recognize the word "hoola." It was probably written by some young computer geek who doesn't know about the finer things in life).

Coffee shops with tableside juke boxes
Home milk delivery in glass bottles, with cardboard stoppers.
> (I used to work for a dairy farmer delivering milk in glass bottles to customers in several New Mexico towns. But before I secured such lucrative employment, I first worked setting pins in a bowling alley. My entrepreneurial colleagues and I would sit behind the pin machine and wait for the bowler to send the bowling ball rolling.

A Funny Thing Happened on My Way to Work . . . I Retired

When they knocked down some pins, we would jump down, pick them up and put them in the holding sleeves. Next, we would pick up their ball and set it on a groove and give it a push. It would roll down a small hill and back up to the bowler. The whole thing would be done again and again. It's amazing that none of us were ever seriously hurt).

Newsreels before the movie
P. F. Flyers
Peashooters
Howdy Doody (Doody-Another word not recognized by spell checker. Those geeks).
Captain Kangaroo
45-RPM Records
Billy don't be a hero
Green Stamps
Hi-fis
Metal ice cube trays with levers
Mimeograph paper
Blue flash bulbs
Roller skate keys
Cork popguns
Drive-ins
The Fuller Brush man
Reel-to-reel tape recorders
The "twist," "mashed potatoes," and "funky-chicken"
Tinker toys
The Erector Set
Lincoln Logs
    (We still have a set that my kids used to play with)
15-cent McDonald hamburgers & 10-cent fries
5 cent packs of baseball cards with that slab of pink bubblegum
Penny candy
Gasoline at 35 cents-a-gallon
When the first man walked on the moon

When the Beatles arrived
Butch wax

NOW FOR A MORE SERIOUS NOSTALGIC STROLL. DO YOU REMEMBER . . . ?

When *pot* was for cooking the evening meal in
When *aids* were helpers in the principles office
You got married first *then* you lived together
When *grass* was something you mowed
When *Spam* was canned meat and not a slew of emails
That being *gay* meant just being happy
When *party lines* were what rural people shared and not a dating service
Software wasn't a word and *hardware* consisted of hammers, nails, etc
The term *terrorist* referred to your little brother who wouldn't leave you alone
Having a *weapon* in school meant being caught with a Sling Shot
The biggest problem for teachers was her student's chewing gum in class
The *Internet* was what lined your swimming trunks
When you went to the *web* to watch a fly get eaten
When *Coke* was a soft drink not something you sniffed
Race issues meant arguing about who ran the fastest
When the *Middle East* referred to Ohio or Indiana
Taking *drugs* meant chewing a Bayer-baby aspirin
Packages weren't sealed for your protection
When *Crack* was something you plastered
When *Home security* was a barking dog or noisy guineas

And my all-time favorite . . . Do you remember when . . . ?

Older siblings were the worst tormentors and the fiercest protectors

A Funny Thing Happened on My Way to Work . . . I Retired

Ok, ok, just one more. I promise: That was then, this is now.

Then	Now
Getting into a new, hip joint	Getting a new hip joint
Hoping for a BMW	Hoping for a BM
Getting your head stoned	Getting your headstone
Acid Rock	Acid Reflux
Popping pills, smoking joints	Popping joints
Trying to look like Marlon Brando and Elizabeth Taylor	Trying *not* to look like Marlon Brando and Elizabeth Taylor

Living through the "boomer" years has enriched us with many historical events. Some events were good and some were anything but good. Since recess is running long I will start with the younger boomers.

1957 **Early boomers are ten years old; late boomers are eight years away from birth. Meanwhile President Eisenhower wins re-election, but Nikita Khrushchev says, "History is on our side. We will bury you!"**
    The Russians launch Sputnik I and Sputnik II; President Eisenhower uses troops to enforce desegregation in Arkansas.

1958 **The U.S. launches the Explorer I satellite; the first Pizza Hut opens.**

1959 **Barbie is "born"; Buddy Holly dies; Castro takes over in Cuba.**

1960 **The soviets shoot down a U.S. spy plane; John Kennedy is elected president; and Chubby Checker introduces the Twist.**

1961 **The Russians and then the U.S. put a man into space; the Berlin wall goes up.**

1962 **K-Mart and Wal-Mart open; Russian warheads in Cuba bring the world to the edge of war.**
1963 **President Kennedy is assassinated; Dr. Martin Luther King declares, "I have a dream."**
1964 **President Johnson declares a "war on poverty." But he also plans the huge escalation of a much larger war to be fought half way around the world. The Beatles "invade" the U.S.**

I hope that this section has brought a smile to your face or even a tear to your eye. In either case, don't ever be in a hurry to get to the next place in your life. During a television interview, an 87-year-old woman was asked, "What were things like in your day?" Smiling, the lady said firmly, "This *is* my day." This is *your* day! History is being made *right now*. Enjoy it.

Ok. Recess is over. Now it's time to go to work. -

"Neither you nor the world know what you can do until you have tried."

-Ralph Waldo Emerson

CHAPTER TWO

TWELVE STEPS TO ATLANTIS

Quite possibly the largest mausoleum in the world is the Taj Mahal. Under construction from 1632 to 1645, that oversized tomb required over 20,000 men during the process of construction. It took 76 years to build the Great Pyramids of Egypt near Cairo. It required seven and a half years for Solomon's temple to be built. Ten thousand men were used for carrying the wood and constructing the temple, and another 20,900 men were used as overseers or supervisors. All three groups of men were involved in a seven and a half year building program for Solomon's temple. As diverse as these three buildings are, the Taj Mahal, the Great Pyramids of Egypt and the Temple of Solomon, there is a truth common to all, for you see, all were built for durability. They were built to stay, and their durability was grounded on rock.

In this chapter we are going to lay the foundation work for a satisfying retirement. We won't be discussing money to a great extent in the next few pages (that will come later in the book) because that is *not* the foundation for a happy retirement. Sometime back, the world stood shocked to learn that the former President of the Philippines, Ferdinand Marcos and his wife, Imelda, had amassed a personal fortune. During his 20-year reign, while their country was devastated by poverty, the Marcos family's wealth grew close to ten billion dollars. And yet with a ten billion dollar empire, they had no place to spend it because no country on the face of God's globe wanted them.

No, my friend, satisfaction must be achieved by another

A Funny Thing Happened on My Way to Work . . . I Retired

source. Following are twelve steps that I believe every retiree needs to climb in order for them to reach *their* City of Atlantis:

In this chapter, we will discover:

TWELVE THINGS YOU CAN DO TO RAISE YOUR OWN LEVEL OF RETIREMENT SATISFACTION

- Think opportunity
- Dream
- Retire and Re-fire
- Bring back Balance
- Find your Strengths
- Get Organized
- Change Negative Talk
- Take a Self-test
- Think Positive Thoughts
- Take Another Self-test
- Take Time to Adjust To Change
- If It Ain't Broke, Break it
- Age Gracefully
- Know What Money Can and Can't Buy

First, let's look at the current level of satisfaction among retirees.

A survey by Allstate Financial of Northbrook, IL found that of 1,004 baby boomers, born between 1946 and 1961, 82 percent believed retirement would be more fun and rewarding than their parent's retirement. Others believe it will be more active (65%) and the best years of their lives (63%).

Today retirement is less about caviar, fishing and travel, and more about borrowing from children, clipping coupons and replacing lobster with tuna as the cuisine of the day *if* we fail to plan.

Admittedly, sustaining your present lifestyle is largely

dependent on the amount of money you have been disciplined enough to save throughout your working years, *but,* the way you handle your retirement event and the way you manage your money afterwards can be equally rewarding or devastating.

In spite of market uncertainty, working people tend to think their retirement lifestyle will be better than their current lifestyle and according to U.S. studies, most retirees *do* indicate a high rate of satisfaction. A study conducted by Williamson, Rinehart, and Blank polled individuals who had been retired for five years and asked them to rate their current level of satisfaction. The results were as follows:

- 68% were very much or somewhat happier
- 20% felt about the same
- 13% were somewhat less or much less happy

According to the study, the retiree's level of satisfaction was influenced by a number of factors:

- White-collar versus blue-collar status. (White-collar workers where generally more satisfied.)
- Whether retirement was voluntary or involuntary
- Financial circumstances
- Personal health (Williamson et al. 1992, pp. 82–85).

"Does this mean if I am a blue-collar worker being forced to retire on less than I wanted to because of back trouble, I won't be happy in retirement?" (Am I too obvious here?) Let me answer that question in **two** ways–first, with an illustration: A man came to church with a long face and a clearly troubled expression. His pastor approached him and asked, "How are you doing today?" His reply was typical, "I'm okay I guess, *under* the circumstances." To which the pastor responded, "What are you doing under there?"

There is no rule that says you have to be *under* circumstances, however, one sure way to stay under there is to make excuses for why you are there in the first place. Life happens. It's not the Republican's fault nor is it the Democrat's fault. One of the greatest ills of our society is the "blame-game." According to the majority of convicted felons, they are either innocent or they are a product of the environment in which they were reared. Granted there are some wrong convictions in our imperfect system, but when a society becomes convinced that it's always the other guy's fault, we find ourselves in a dangerous quagmire. It starts to sound like the little boy who was caught fighting. When asked what happened, his excuse was: "He started it when he hit me back!" Deep down we know that the responsibility of our lives rests with us, yet it seems when "accidents" happen it is always the other guy's fault. I've listed some actual insurance claims taken from company files to illustrate the folly behind this kind of rationale.

- "The other car collided with mine without giving warning of its intentions."
- "An invisible car came out of nowhere, struck my vehicle and vanished."
- "I'd been driving for forty years, when I fell asleep at the wheel and had an accident."
- "A pedestrian hit me and went under my car."
- "Coming home, I drove into the wrong house and collided with a tree I don't have."
- "As I approached the intersection, a sign suddenly appeared in a place where no sign had ever been before. So I was unable to stop in time to avoid an accident."
- "The pedestrian had no idea which direction to run, so I ran over him."
- "The telephone pole was approaching. I was attempting to swerve out of the way when it struck my front end."
- "As I reached the intersection, a hedge sprang up, obscuring my vision. I just didn't see the other car."

- "The guy was all over the road, and I had to swerve a number of times before hitting him."
- My car was legally parked when it backed into the other vehicle."

(And my all-time favorite):
- "I pulled away from the side of the road, glanced at my mother-in-law and headed over the embankment."

Do you see the desperate struggle to justify why we are weak and imperfect? The fact is, it's okay to be faulty. I like being around imperfect people because my quirks and failures are less noticeable around them. I know I've been riding the soapbox pretty hard these last few lines but I think it is important for you and me to see life for what it is. Life, as well as retirement, is what *you* make it.

Now, before you say, "That may be true, but you don't know my situation. What can I do to improve my circumstances?" Let me offer the second answer I promised earlier. I've included twelve practical suggestions that you can implement today which can greatly raise your level of fulfillment in retirement and life in general. Some of these suggestions are going to get pretty personal and some are going to seem downright impossible to do. Don't get discouraged by thinking you are doomed to live life "under the circumstances" just because the tasks seem out of reach. At first, some of these tasks will make you feel like what I have asked you to do is unreasonable; give it time, give it time.

TWELVE THINGS YOU CAN DO *RIGHT NOW* TO RAISE YOUR OWN LEVEL OF RETIREMENT SATISFACTION

1. THINK OPPORTUNITY:

Think of your retirement as an opportunity to move from one level of life to another, not as an unavoidable necessity like taxes. It's important to start the transition with the right perspective and with the right frame of mind. This mental adjustment will influence everything else you do with regards to your retirement and life. Some think, erroneously, that retirement is a step down into second-class status. While it indeed is a step, it is not down but up. One phase of life has ended and another phase has begun for the retiree. A phase that they have never experienced before.

Porris Wittel, a dockworker in Gillingham, England hated his alarm clock for 47 years. For 47 years that thing jangled him awake. On the day of his retirement he got his revenge. He took his alarm clock to work and he flattened it in an eighty-ton hydraulic press. He said, "It was a lovely feeling."

Think of your retirement as an opportunity to experience that "lovely feeling." Go crush your alarm clock.

2. DREAM:

Begin to dream and plan to accomplish things that were impossible during your working years. If you had the time and money to do anything you wanted to do, what would it be? What have you always wanted to do? Where have you always wanted to go? Don't surround your ideas with realistic boundaries, instead brainstorm the impossible and then find a way to make it possible. Dare to dream, take risks. Don't create imaginary walls that hold you back from your goals.

Raynald III was a fourteenth-century duke in what is now Belgium. Raynald was grossly overweight. Captured in a revolt by his younger brother, he was imprisoned in a room that was built around him. The room had no bars on the windows—not even a locked door, though the door was slightly smaller than normal. Unfortunately, because of his size, he could not squeeze through to freedom. He was too large. Still there was hope. All he had to do to be a free man was to go on a diet. His brother even offered to restore his title and wealth as soon as he was able to leave the room.

His brother knew Raynald's weakness, though. Each day he had sent to Raynald's room a variety of delicious foods. Instead of growing thinner, Raynald grew fatter. He was a prisoner, not of locks or bars or iron gates, *but of his own appetite.*

Dare to dream. Don't be a prisoner of your own fears. The whole world is waiting for you.

3. RETIRE AND RE-FIRE:

Do you want to go back to school or start a new business? The primary reason a new business fails is due to lack of working capital. In other words, more money is going out than is coming in. I can't think of a better time to start a new business than after retirement when you're income is predictable.

A well-known person reluctantly accepted retirement and became anxious and depressed. However he had a dream about opening a fried chicken restaurant using a recipe that had been in the family for years. Colonel Sanders and his Kentucky Fried Chicken franchises are now part of the landscape in nearly every populated area. Go for it Colonel!

Someone once said, "It's always too early to quit." Retirement is not about quitting, it is about changing direction. In fact, many retirees find themselves in better shape than they were in pre-retirement years due to a healthier diet and a more active lifestyle. I spend most of my day sitting behind a desk. My greatest exertion used to be answering the telephone until my wife encouraged me to walk everyday after lunch. Sometimes, when I get home, I feel too tired to do anything physical.

A Funny Thing Happened on My Way to Work . . . I Retired

This may sound like a copout to you but I remember what an old preacher in Atoka, Oklahoma once told me. Reverend Crowson said, "You can work eight hours in the field hauling bales of hay and I can work eight hours visiting the sick and shut-ins and I guarantee you we will both be just as tired at the end of the day."

When retirement comes, discipline yourself, get active and stay active. Don't skip a beat. Beware of taking a few weeks to unwind. Inertia can set in pretty quickly and "a body at rest, tends to stay at rest." Stay in motion.

Three elderly men were discussing the type of accidental death each would prefer.

One man, who must have been in his seventies, said, "I would prefer a quick death, like an airplane crash." The second man, who was around eighty years old, said, "Let me drown to death in the sea." Finally the man in his nineties, after a few moments reflection, said, "I would like to be shot by a jealous husband." That may not be the best way to go but you can't deny the fact that this man is on fire!

My lovely wife, Alice, and I were married in her hometown of Lewisville, Arkansas. When the wedding ceremony was over, we made the traditional dash for the car under a shower of birdseed. (After all, we gotta keep PETA off our backs). Just before we reached the car, an old woman came up to Alice and said, "Honey, you'll be back home in two weeks!" Hmmm. That was eighteen years ago this month. I guess that sweet little 'ol *busybody* was wrong. People will "warn" you not to dream too big when what they are really saying is, "Don't reach new heights in life because I am too afraid to try and I don't want to be left down here alone."

Professional speaker, Joe Larson, once said, "My friends didn't believe that I could become a successful speaker. So I did something about it. I went out and found me some new friends!"

When you are ready to re-fire your life, people will surround you telling you there are 28 reasons why, whatever it is you want to do, won't work. Some will say, "You'll come crawling back in two weeks begging for your old job back." Others will tell you that you don't know any other kind of trade and to consider starting a new business would be foolish and irresponsible–"I know a friend, who knows a friend, who knows this guy who tried to start a business recapping shoestrings with that little plastic tip, and he didn't make it." If I listened to my negative "friends" when they told me I couldn't start my own investment firm, I would still be working a nine to fiver in a mid-level job doing mediocre work for someone else. Instead, I am pursuing an extremely satisfying career in investments AND I am privileged to write this book. What I did was simply surround myself with positive friends. I'm not advocating you envelop yourself with "yes" men, rather, find those people who are encouragers by nature and you will draw strength from their positive attitude. This is true in all walks of life but it is essential when making a major life change.

So, what should you do in a situation where your friends, with good intentions, try to discourage you from coloring outside the lines? Let's draw from the deep pool of historical experience for this answer. Let's do what Alexander the Great did.

In between conquering campaigns, Alexander the Great would pause and gather his men around him. He would reward those who were faithful and courageous and punish those who were cowardly and dishonest. During one of these respite occasions, a young boy was brought before this valiant leader. The charge was read that the boy panicked, deserted his post, and hid in a cave during a heated battle. When Alexander the Great looked at the boy's young, innocent face, he was moved and felt compassion for him. In a tender voice he said, "Young man, what is your name?" Almost as a whisper the boy said, "Alexander." The kindness melted away from Alexander the Great's face. He asked again, but this time with a sterner tone, "What did you say your name was?" The boy again responded hoarsly,

"Alexander, sir." The great leader stood up, pointed his finder at the young lad and said, "Boy! Change your conduct, or change your name!"

True friends won't try to tear you down; they will try to build you up. If they habitually ridicule and mock your ideas and efforts, tell them to change their conduct or you change the name . . . of your "friends."

4. BRING BACK BALANCE:

Realize retirement is an opportunity to bring balance into your life. We are complex creatures made up of many different relational parts such as family, social relationships, physical needs, mental faculties, faith, and values. With only so many hours in a day, it is impossible to afford appropriate time to each area. More than likely, several of these areas have been neglected due to the demanding schedule placed on us by work. Retirement is an excellent time to rediscover dormant areas in our lives that make us who we are.

When my mother retired from the State Highway Department in New Mexico, she did something that she wanted to do ever since we made the move from our 70-acre farm in Indiana. She bought an 85-acre ranch. After much encouragement from yours truly, she purchased several head of cattle that she still raises today.

A study by Bryn Mawr College sixty years ago discovered that women of that day devoted more than eighty hours a week to cleaning the house, cooking meals, and taking care of the children. Did things get better? You know the answer to that.

Another study twenty-five years later reported that full-time housewives spent more hours doing laundry in the 1970s than they did in the 1920s, despite all the new washing machines, dryers, detergents, and bleaches. Why? The main reason for the increase was due to families acquiring more clothing, and because they had even higher expectations about cleanliness and grooming.

Today few women can even afford dreaming of devoting full-time to their families. Thus the extraordinary demands of running a home are added to running an office or a classroom or a business. And then came retirement.

What sacrifices did you make to provide for your family? Now is the time to pursue those desires again. You've earned it.

5. FIND YOUR STRENGTH:

Find out what your strengths are and build on them. Develop goals and priorities in each area of your life to help organize your time and energies. Goals create action and its action that gets results. One of the reasons people often become dissatisfied with retirement is they don't have specific, measurable goals. As my good friend, Weldon Wynn said, "When you see a hill ahead, look past it to the other side and prepare to meet what lies in the valley." Don't set goals that are too easy to attain, rather, set goals beyond what you can see and begin the journey toward a loftier place.

Remember, it hasn't been your nature to do nothing. You are used to an active lifestyle and sudden change can feel unnatural. Author, Henri Nouwen told the story of an old man who used to meditate early every morning under a big tree on the bank of the Ganges River. One morning the old man saw a scorpion floating helplessly in the water. As the scorpion was washed closer to the tree, the old man reached out to rescue the drowning creature. As soon as he touched it, however, the scorpion stung him. Instinctively the man withdrew his hand. A minute later, though, he tried again. This time the scorpion stung him so badly with its poisonous tail that the man's hand became swollen and bloody and his face contorted with pain.

At that moment, a passerby saw the old man struggling with the scorpion and shouted: "Hey, stupid old man, what's wrong with you? Only a fool would risk his life for the sake of an ugly, evil creature. Don't you know you could kill yourself trying to save that ungrateful scorpion?"

Looking into the stranger's eyes the old man said calmly, "My friend, just because it is the scorpion's nature to sting, that does not change my nature to save." (Brennan Manning, THE SIGNATURE OF JESUS, Old Tappan N.J.: Fleming H. Revell, 1988)

Find what it is in your nature that makes you who you are and build on it. Don't try to be something you're not. Don't let time become something just to fill in, instead let it be something that brings you closer to your hopes and dreams.

6. GET ORGANIZED:

Organize your time and get a day planner because, after a life of hard work and stress it is easy to lapse into doing things that are impulse driven. It's healthy to be spontaneous but only sparingly. As someone once said, "Life is what goes on while we're doing other things." Don't let it go on without you. Keep growing. You know the old saying, "If you rest you rust."

Many years ago, the captain of a whaling vessel in the North Atlantic spotted through his binoculars the hull of a ship, which was obviously very old and run down and surrounded by icebergs.

As the captain's vessel approached the ship, his crew's cries of "Ship Ahoy!" were met with no response. Going aboard the vessel, the boarding party found the entire crew frozen, but well preserved. The captain of this icy vessel was fully dressed and sat before his logbook at his desk. The last entry revealed that these men had been adrift for almost ten years, far removed from ocean traffic in the cold, icy waters of the north. The crew of the whaling vessel had discovered a floating sepulcher surrounded by icebergs, adrift on an ocean with nowhere to go.

When you retire, have somewhere to go. Direction takes planning. Planning takes organization. If you don't want to stagnate your retirement years, get organized. When you come up with a plan, stick to it. The story is told of a bloodhound, which started a hunt chasing a stag. A fox crossed the path, so the hound chased the fox. After a while a rabbit crossed the path, so the hound chased it. Later, a mouse crossed the path, and the hound chased the mouse into a hole. The hound began his hunt on the trail of a magnificent stag, and he ended up watching a mouse hole. Organization is the difference between pursuing a stag and staring at a mouse hole. Get organized.

7. CHANGE NEGATIVE TALK:

If you keep saying bad things are going to happen, you run the risk of becoming a prophet. Eliminate negative self-talk because it works against a successful transition into retirement. If you listen to country music you know it's about losing. What do you get when you play country music backwards? You get your truck back, you get your dog back, you get your girl back, etc. Sometimes we don't need to unwind as much as we need to rewind. We need to go back and find what it is that causes us to dwell on negative thoughts and correct it. Richard P. Johnson, Ph. D., lists ten negative attitudes that can be harmful to your retirement psyche. Place an "X" beside the ones you are struggling with:

1. ___ Retirement is an immediate, usually irrevocable, descent into second-class citizenship.
2. ___ America doesn't like retired people.
3. ___ Families don't want retired people.
4. ___ Retired people are of interest only to doctors, real estate people, and travel agents.
5. ___ Retired people are only valued for the money they command.
6. ___ Retirees want to "belong" but they can do so only with their own kind.
7. ___ Retirement means that you have one foot in the grave.

8. ___ The activities of older persons are only meaningless fillers.
9. ___ There is something suicidal about retirement.
10. ___ To be retired is to be regarded as incompetent.

Look at the areas you checked. Discuss these with your spouse, or a close friend or your pastor. Find someone who will listen to you. Don't leave these issues unattended. You don't have to accept these false thought patterns one second longer. It won't be easy, but it will be worth the effort to change the way you think about things. You will have to face negative thoughts every day, but, with practice, you can begin to see things as they really are. As M. Scott Peck said in the first line of his book, *The Road Less Traveled,* "Life is difficult." Since we already know this to be true, we can be better equipped to deal with unconstructive thinking when it trys to block our path. This leads us into the next truth.

8. THINK POSITIVE THOUGHTS:

Remember the song, "Don't Worry, Be Happy"? Silly yes, but profound. Don't be a member of the Hurry-Worry-Bury Club. Dr. Johnson goes on to list positive attitudes that can greatly enhance your level of satisfaction in retirement. Put an "X" by the ones you currently possess and an "N" by the ones you need to improve on.

1. ___ Life is becoming truly exciting for me now that I am retired. I'm learning the job of taking control of my own life.
2. ___ I have decided to let go of those things that I have allowed to keep me from genuinely growing before I retired.
3. ___ I now concentrate on those things that help me to take hold of myself, focus my efforts, and

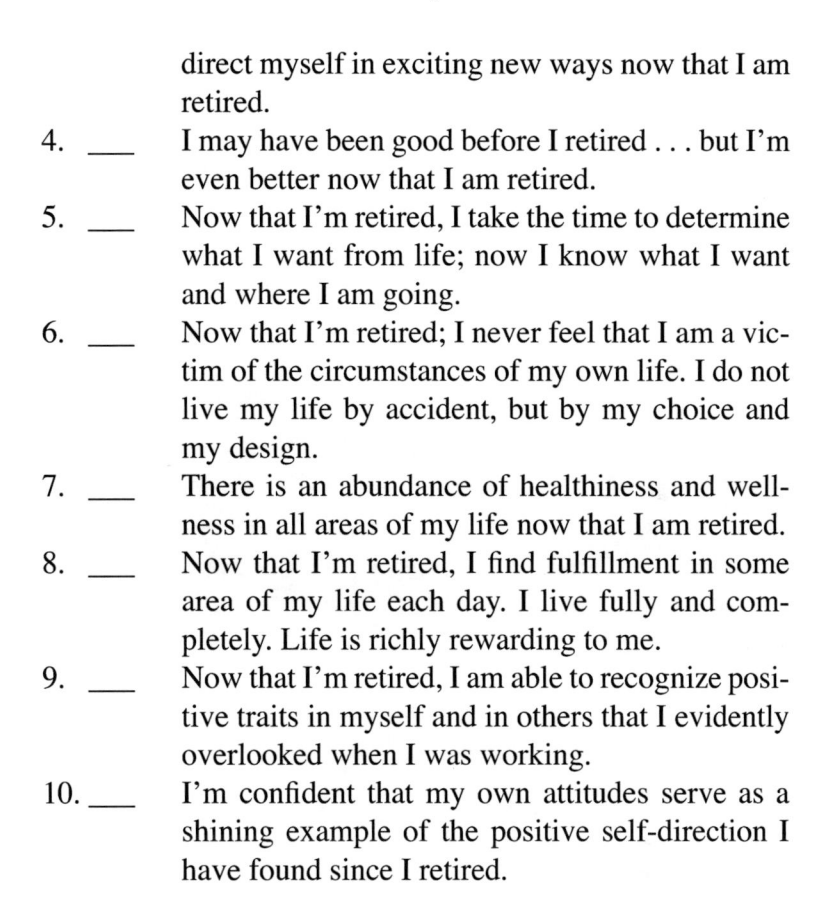

direct myself in exciting new ways now that I am retired.
4. ___ I may have been good before I retired . . . but I'm even better now that I am retired.
5. ___ Now that I'm retired, I take the time to determine what I want from life; now I know what I want and where I am going.
6. ___ Now that I'm retired; I never feel that I am a victim of the circumstances of my own life. I do not live my life by accident, but by my choice and my design.
7. ___ There is an abundance of healthiness and wellness in all areas of my life now that I am retired.
8. ___ Now that I'm retired, I find fulfillment in some area of my life each day. I live fully and completely. Life is richly rewarding to me.
9. ___ Now that I'm retired, I am able to recognize positive traits in myself and in others that I evidently overlooked when I was working.
10. ___ I'm confident that my own attitudes serve as a shining example of the positive self-direction I have found since I retired.

Don't dismiss the threat of depression when retirement is in full bloom. Depression after a major event, even a *good* one, can and does happen. Be prepared to deal with this all-to-common occurrence. Many times it is temporary, but sometimes it can be prolonged and if not dealt with correctly, can be devastating.

It is estimated that 58,000 American soldiers died in the Vietnam conflict. As bad as those numbers are, the survivors faced another war when they returned home. Since that time, it is estimated that over 60,000 Vietnam veterans have committed suicide. When you come home from work for the last time you might find yourself in a war of hope vs. despair, love vs. hatred, energy vs. lethargy. Prepare to do what it takes to win this war.

9. TAKE TIME TO ADJUST TO CHANGE:

When Harry and Ada Mae had Sandra, their first child, they had to travel 200 miles to El Paso, Texas, for the delivery. When they brought Sandra home, it was to their ranch on the Arizona/New Mexico border, where life was not easy. Their little adobe home had no electricity or running water. There was no school within driving distance. With such limited resources, anyone would have thought that Sandra's future was not bright.

When Sandra was four, her mother began her education at home. She looked on it as a never-ending job, reading to Sandra hour after hour. Later, Sandra was sent to the best boarding schools that the family could afford because they wanted her to go on to college. Her father, Harry, had been frustrated in his ambition to attend Stanford University. His father had died just before he was to enter Stanford, and he had been forced to take over the ranch.

But Sandra did go to Stanford, then on to law school. Most of us know her as Sandra Day O'Connor-the first woman Supreme Court justice in the United States.

It goes to show you can't judge a person just by their beginnings. The same is true about your retirement. Don't judge the future of it based on its beginnings. Good or bad.

The transition from rat racing to turtle walking is often a jarring and unsettling experience. One doesn't move seamlessly and painlessly from one stage to the other. There will be periods of uncertainty, anxiety, even fear. Give yourself time to make the adjustment. I've talked with clients and prospects that said they tried retirement for a few days and couldn't stand it so they found another job. Although there is nothing wrong with working after retirement, it is a good idea to allow yourself time to adjust to the change before taking on more responsibility. Too many changes in a short period of time can raise stress levels disproportionately. Avoid this if at all possible.

For many, retirement is like leaving a family. Russell Dalby worked on an assembly line for many years. His job was very monotonous. Work was long, sometimes boring, and often tiring. What made it bearable were the people he worked with day in and day out. They became his friends. He experienced a sense of community with them.

Russell described many after-work activities that he and other co-workers participated in; pot lucks, Christmas and Thanksgiving dinners, as well as other memorable festivities. There were times when the co-workers celebrated a new birth. There were times when people were sick and in the hospital and people at work responded. When someone came to work who experienced a tragedy in their life, everyone would pull together for them, offering help in many forms.

Russell has retired. He misses his co-workers a lot. He still remembers their names and birthdays. They are a very special part of his life.

We tend to try and replace lost or broken relationships with busyness. It doesn't work. Cultivating existing relationships and building new ones is the best antidote to pain of this kind. Don't let yourself go home and mope around the house for days, pining away for your former comrades. Ponder their memories and if possible, keep in contact with them, but don't do this at the neglect and expense of your family and friends who are there for you right now.

Accept the fact that resisting change is natural. Most of us resist change even when it is in our best interest. The standard typewriter keyboard (which I am typing on right now) is a good example of that. Have you ever noticed where the most frequently used keys are located? They're placed as far apart as possible. The original purpose of this arrangement was to slow down typing speed. Keys on the machines of the 1800s used to jam if the typist went too fast. About 50 years ago, a keyboard

A Funny Thing Happened on My Way to Work . . . I Retired

called the Dvorak Simplified Keyboard was developed. On this keyboard, the most frequently used keys are in the home row, and the right hand does more of the work (56 percent) than the left. Tests show that typists can greatly increase their speed (up to five times) with no increase in errors. Yet, we still labor on with a keyboard designed to be inefficient. Why? We don't like to change.

Many psychologists agree that any change, whether it is good or bad, produces stress. We naturally try to avoid stress, even when it is obvious that the change will be good for us. Going from an environment of structure and demand to a sudden stop in activity can be extremely stressful. Moving too quickly into another job can add unnecessary stress to an already volatile situation. I have seen workers retire and then, almost immediately, start another job. Almost all of these individuals quit their new job in a matter of weeks. Give yourself time to adjust. How much time is needed is of course up to the individual, but time is now your friend so take all of it you need to assimilate.

Do you remember years ago on TV when THE WIDE WORLD OF SPORTS television program came on? The announcer would say the infamous words, "The thrill of victory, and *the agony of defeat.*" Remember the skier as he appeared to come down the hill in good form, then, suddenly, for no apparent reason, falls, bounces off the supporting structure, and flies into a tailspin? Didn't you just ache for the man?

"What viewers didn't know was that he *chose* to fall rather than finish the jump. Why you ask? As he explained later, the jump surface had become too fast, and midway down, he realized if he completed the jump, he would touch down on the level ground, beyond the safe landing area, which could have proved fatal. As it was, the skier suffered no more than a headache from the tumble.

It's really hard to change, but it's better than a fatal landing. We can change if we really want to. A good friend of mine who is a marriage counselor tells his patients, "Action leads to feeling." I have found this phrase to be absolutely true. How many times have you dreaded going to a party or a ballgame, only to find out that you had a wonderful time? We shouldn't *feel* our way into *acting,* but rather *act* our way into *feeling*. Sometimes we need to do the action, trusting that the feeling will come later.

10. IF IT AIN'T BROKE, BREAK IT! (THE MOLD THAT IS):

When Ricky Ricardo would come home he would sometimes say in his Cuban accent, "Lucy, you got some 'splainin to do." When you get home it will be more like "Lucy, you got some 'justin to do." When you come home for good from your job you and your spouse are going to have some serious *adjusting* to do. It will be time to break some outdated molds. This won't be easy since change of this magnitude is very difficult, but it's not impossible.

Several years ago, when the Denver Zoo was going through major renovations, a polar bear arrived before its naturalistic environment was ready for habitation. The temporary cage that it was put in was just big enough for the large animal to take three nice, swinging steps in one direction, whirl up and around, come back down and take three steps in the other direction. The polar bear went back and forth, day after day for many, many months in that constraining setting with those bars constantly restricting its movement. Eventually, a naturalistic environment was built around this cage, on-site. When it was finally completed, the cage was removed from around the polar bear. Guess what happened? That's right. It still paced back and forth as if the cage were still there. (Richard Bandler and John Grinder, Frogs Into Princes Moab. Utah: Real People press 1979), p.192)

You've been doing the same thing for so long it has become an extension of your life. Even if you hated your job and couldn't wait to get away from it, you will still have to go through some serious adjustments.

Years ago I had to go under the knife to straighten a deviated septum in the bridge of my nose. To fix it, the surgeon had to first break the cartilage in my nose then re-set it so it would be straight. That was the worst five days of recovery I have ever experienced. However, I have been able to breathe freely through my nose for eighteen years. The pain was worth it! You may have to "break" some habits to adjust to your new schedule and it could be painful emotionally, mentally, and even physically, but you will be able to "breathe" when you heal. Get out the hammer and chisel and get to breakin.'

11. AGE GRACEFULLY:

Age successfully. What do I mean by this? As we begin to recognize retirement as simply another event occurring in our life, much like our wedding and career choice was, we begin to understand the fact that we can control many aspects of it. While it is true you can't stop the aging process, it is also true you can maintain a fulfilling lifestyle in spite of circumstances beyond your control. Some of you reading this may have already begun to see physical maladies creeping in. Even with the advances in medicine, aging is unstoppable but *not* unbearable. How so? By aging successfully.

A person who ages successfully will:

- *Remain physically, socially and mentally active.*

Some people make excuses, as they get older claiming they're too old to try something new or too old to handle something new. Ruth Rothfarb probably won't sympathize. At age 72, she decided to *start* running for exercise. At age 80, she entered her first marathon (26.2 miles). By age 89, she had run 10 marathons! Ruth claims that she has the same aches and pains that everyone her age experiences but says that running keeps her healthy and distracts her from the aches.

As you can see there is more to retirement than fishing and playing golf. Look into community opportunities. Join the traveling Bar-B-Q circuit where people compete for prizes based on their cooking abilities. Find an old junk car and learn how to restore it. Join a motorcycle club. Run a marathon. You get the idea.

* *Compensate for age-related changes.*

Remember Gracie Allen, who played the scatterbrained wife in a comedy team with her husband George Burns? In one routine, Gracie called in a repairman to fix her electric clock. The repairman fiddled with it for a while and then told her, "There's nothing wrong with the clock; you just didn't have it plugged in." Gracie replied, "I don't want to waste electricity, so I only plug it in when I want to know what time it is."

Wouldn't it be nice if we could simply unplug from the aging process every once in a while? Unfortunately reality won't let us and so we keep getting older. When you find that you can't do things as well as you once did, don't quit! Compensate! Look for the alternative. If you can't play softball any more, coach it. (I coach my daughter's fast pitch team and love it). If you can't run, walk. If you can't play golf (I'm dangerous with a golf club), then play bingo. If you can't play, work.

When I discuss things like this I am reminded of a funny story I heard when I was in Seminary. There was an old black cotton picker working in the hot sun. One day his back was hurting, the sun was beating down on him, he was tired and thirsty and just plain worn out. He finally turned to his companion and said, "If it gets any hotter, I swear I'm going to hear God call me to preach!" At least the cotton-picker wasn't willing to quit working; he just wanted a change of vocation. Don't quit; compensate.

* *Accept aging as a natural part of life.*

In the comic, *Dennis the Menace,* Mr. Wilson tells Dennis that he (Mr. Wilson), was once just like him. Dennis can't wait to share this with his friend Joey. He explains to Joey that Mr. Wilson got dirty and had fights and stole cookies and broke things, etc., just the way Dennis did. To which his friend replies, "Gee! He sounds like a regular fella! I wonder where he went wrong?"

Where do some people go wrong? When they refuse to accept aging as a part of life. This is a serious mistake. It is both amusing and sad to see so many "fountain of youth" products hit the market every day. The American Society of Plastic and Reconstructive surgeons estimates that 2800 certified surgeons annually perform 477,000 "esthetic" operations: optional procedures to make people look and feel better. (By the way, this survey was conducted in 1992. I didn't have room to put today's numbers in the book. (Just kidding).

Remember, every young person will someday be an old person (if they are fortunate). I'm certainly not advocating that you stop taking care of yourself. If a miracle-cream can bleach away those age spots, great. Just learn to roll with the punches. Phyllis Diller said she was in a beauty contest once. "I not only came in last," she said, "I was hit in the mouth by Miss Congeniality" . . . Roll.

- *Have a sense of control over their lives.*

As I have said, money can't buy happiness, but it can give you choices. Having choices means having control. We all like being in control to a certain degree. Here are some funny "mistakes" people make while traveling.

WORDS WE WISH WE'D NEVER SAID

- "Sure we'll take the dog along. How much trouble can it be?"
- "The car needs a tune-up, but we can get one on the road. They cost about the same everywhere."
- "The heck with reservations! We're sure to find a place."

- "I know we only have a quarter tank of gas, but there's bound to be one or two stations along this shortcut."
- "The suntan lotion is up in our room; but another half hour won't hurt."
- "Aw, c'mon! A little French place like this couldn't be too expensive!"
- "We'll get the flat fixed where we stop for the night. I never heard of two tires going bad in one day."

As I said, control means choices. These people had choices with each situation and they chose chance and assumption as their path. Oops! Whatever you do, don't assume things will just "work out." Remember Murphy's Law. Take control and stay in the driver's seat.

- *Generally view change as a challenge rather than a threat.*

Change is inevitable, but it doesn't have to be intolerable. We are all creatures of habit but we are also quick to adapt to our surroundings. Early on in our marriage, my wife and I moved three times in as many years. When we moved into a new house, I would feel lost for the first few weeks because of the strange surroundings. After awhile though, the house began to feel like home. Give it time. Retirement will begin to feel like home. Again, give it time. You will find the adjustment gets easier as time goes on.

After every big storm plenty of broken oak limbs can be found lying on the ground. But you never find any branches from the fir trees. Oak trees are big and strong, but they stand stiff and straight. When the wind blows, they crack. But fir trees sway with the storm, and snap back afterward. Just remember; if you want to be king of the forest, you can't be too proud to *bend with the wind,* otherwise you might be "Gone With The Wind."

If you do have to lower your standard of living due to financial hardships during retirement, you will face the choice

A Funny Thing Happened on My Way to Work . . . I Retired

of bending or breaking. In a situation like this you have two basic options: 1. Go back to work (if you are physically able) or, 2. Adjust your spending to compensate for the lowered income. Neither choice means the death of a happy retirement. Learn to bend with the wind no matter which way it chooses to blow.

> *One ship drives east, and another west*
> *With the self-same winds that blow:*
> *Like the winds of the sea are the ways of fate,*
> *As they voyage along through life;*
> *"Tis the will of the soul*
> *That decides its goal,*
> *And not the calm or the strife*
>
> -Ella Wheeler Wilcox

◆ *Accept who they are.*

I've heard parents tell their children before a competition: "You don't have to be first, just don't be last." What if you *are* last? Accept your limitations and expound on your strengths and abilities. No one is good at everything, but everybody is good at something. One of my favorite hobbies is building houses. I learned how to build houses after graduate school because I wanted to build my own house. I can dig and pour the footing, frame the house, roof it, plumb it, wire it, sheetrock it, float it and paint it. However, I can't build cabinets. No way, no how. I can swing a framing hammer but I'm terrible with a finish hammer. There is no way I can cut two pieces of wood and seamlessly join them together. Does that mean I can't build a house because I can't complete it? No. I accept the fact that I'm not a finisher. I hire out that phase of the building process to someone who is. Accept who you are and what you can do and "hire" out the rest.

Another very important aspect of accepting who you are

is by not trying to keep up with the Joneses. You will never catch them.

An MG Midget pulled alongside a Rolls Royce at a traffic light. "Do you have a car phone?" its driver asked the guy in the Rolls. "Of course I do," replied the haughty deluxe-car driver. "Well, do you have a fax machine?" asked the Midget driver. The driver in the Rolls sighed. "I have that, too." "Then do you have a double bed in the back?" The Midget driver wanted to know. Ashen-faced, the Rolls driver sped off. That afternoon, he had a double bed installed in his auto. A week later, the Rolls driver passed the same MG Midget, which was parked on the side of the road—back windows fogged up and steam pouring out. The driver pulled over, got out of the Rolls and banged on the MG's back window until the driver stuck his head out. "I want you to know that I had a double bed installed," bragged the Rolls driver. The MG driver was unimpressed and dripping wet. "You got me out of the shower to tell me that?"

Accept who you are and what you have because as soon as you catch up with the Joneses, they will refinance and pull away again.

- *Remain interested in the world around them, stretch their minds, and maintain an interest in others.*

Now might be a good time in your life to delve into politics on a local or even national level. I know what you're thinking; you couldn't do something like that. What qualifications do *you* bring to the table?

Once, years ago, there was a little girl in an institution who was almost like a wild beast. The workers at the institution had written her off as hopeless. But an elderly nurse believed there was hope for the child. She felt she could communicate love and hope to this wild little creature. The nurse daily visited the child whom they called little Annie, but for a long time little Annie gave no indication she was aware of her presence. The elderly nurse persisted and repeatedly brought some cook-

A Funny Thing Happened on My Way to Work . . . I Retired

ies and left them in her room. Soon the doctors in the institution noticed a change. After a period of time, they moved little Annie upstairs. Finally, the day came when this seemingly "hopeless case" was released. Filled with compassion for others because of her institution experience, little Annie . . . Ann Sullivan wanted to help others.

It was Anne Sullivan who, in turn, played the crucial role in the life of Helen Keller. It was she who saw the great potential in this little blind, deaf and rebellious child. Annie loved Helen, disciplined her, played, prayed, pushed, and worked with her until Helen Keller became an inspiration to the entire world.

But it all began with a nurse whose only qualification was love and compassion. You say you are not qualified? I seriously doubt it. Stay involved. We need your attributes. George Washington Carver once said, "No individual has any right to come into the world and go out of it without leaving behind him distinct and legitimate reasons for having passed through it."

- *Look ahead and set goals for the future.*

Be a visionary. The danger is not setting the goal too high and missing the mark, the real danger is setting the goal to low and hitting the mark. Sometimes goals seem unreachable but we have to try.

There was a high school swimmer a few years back named Nelson. Nelson dreamed of one day making it to the Olympics. He was a lifeguard at his high school pool. One day when no one was around, he got bored. He thought it would be cool to jump into the pool from high up on the spectator's balcony. Unfortunately, he slipped just as he was starting his dive and fell short of the pool, shattering both hands and wrists on the surrounding deck. Now he has pins holding his hands and wrists together. Doctors told him he would probably never swim again.

It was a devastating time for young Nelson. But Nelson had a coach named Chris who refused to give up on his potential as a swimmer. He made him get back in the water as soon as the casts were off his arms, even though Nelson could not yet swim a lick. He pushed Nelson to work first his legs and then his arms back into condition. Late one afternoon Nelson told the coach he was too tired to go on. Chris, his coach, said nothing. He simply pulled all the ladders out of the pool, turned out the lights and left.

He left Nelson alone in the pool. The only way Nelson could get out of the water without using his fragile wrists was to hook his elbows through the rungs of a ladder, and now there were no ladders. In order to stay afloat, Nelson had to keep kicking. Twenty minutes later, Chris returned and put the ladders back in the water. The coach proved again that Nelson could do more than he thought he could. A few weeks later, Nelson was swimming. The conclusion to the story is that Nelson Diebold won the gold medal in Barcelona in 1992.

Now before you get too mad at Chris, Nelson learned later that while he was thrashing helplessly in the water that day with the ladders pulled out and the lights turned off, his coach had been watching him from the spectators' balcony. As frightened as he was, he wasn't alone.

Do I expect you to set a goal for the gold at the next Olympics? Maybe.

- *Learn from your mistakes.*

If you are making mistakes, CONGRATULATIONS! No one ever succeeded without making mistakes. Mistakes happen all through life. I know it is never easy to admit to or accept the errors and failures of our past. I bet if I offered you a way to go back in time and undo some of those mistakes, you would do it with little hesitation. I don't think there is anyone in his or her right mind that wouldn't take advantage of such an offer. But the problem is we can't go back so we must learn from our errors. Failure is not falling down. Failure is falling down and refusing to get back up. That great coach, Vince Lombardi once said, "It's not whether you get knocked down. It's whether you get up again."

Even if you are not a football or baseball buff, I'll bet you recognize the name Mickey Mantle. Did you know that Mickey Mantle experienced 1,710 strikeouts and 1,734 walks during his career with the New York Yankees? That's 3,444 times that he came to bat without hitting the ball. If a man playing regularly gets around 500 at-bats per season, then Mantle played seven years without ever hitting the ball! Folks, that's what I call falling down and getting back up.

Persistence pays off, but keep in mind that there may be times when repeated failures means we need to try something new. That's part of learning from our mistakes.

There is a story of two hunters who flew deep into remote Canada in search of elk. When they started back home, their pilot, seeing that they had bagged six elk, told them the plane could carry only four out. The hunters protested. "The plane that carried us out last year was exactly like this one. The horsepower was the same, the weather was similar, and we had six elk then." Hearing this, the pilot reluctantly agreed to try. They loaded up and took off. Unfortunately the plane did not have sufficient power to climb out of the valley with all that weight, so they crashed. As they stumbled from the wreckage, one hunter asked the other if he knew where they were. "Well, I'm not sure," replied the second hunter, "but I think we are about two miles from where we crashed last year."

Some people are hopeless. They never learn. But you and I are smarter than that aren't we? We can learn from past experiences. We can sit down, think things out and come to some logical conclusions. All we have to do is use our brains. Psychologists tell us that about 10,000 thoughts pass through the human brain each day. That makes 70,000 each week and 3.65 million thoughts a year. One or two of them ought to take. Learn from past mistakes.

One important assumption on my part in this section is

that you have made some mistakes in your life. The person who is not failing is the person who is not trying. You can't learn from mistakes you don't make. My whole point here is to learn, not to avoid making mistakes. A novice sailor supposedly asked a veteran skipper how he learned the positions of Chesapeake Bay's many shoals and bars. The reply: "Hit 'em all!"

- *Choose a healthy lifestyle.*

I had a professor in graduate school that said the only exercise he would ever be caught doing would be walking as a pallbearer for one of his colleagues who exercised too much. Don't be quite that extreme. I hate to run. I get bored running for no purpose; consequently, I won't stay with a running program. I do like to build and I like sports. I'll stay with those things longer. If you don't like walking every morning, go swimming or join a hunting club. Ride a bike. Walk the golf course. Find what you enjoy and you will find it easy to stick with it. You know the saying, "Find a job you love and you'll never work another day in your life." The same is true of exercise. To be prudent, talk to your doctor before engaging in any exerting activities.

If you were a fast-food junkie during your working days, you have some changes to make. The word I want to stress here is not abstinence, but temperance. You may be a big believer in the low-carb craze and that's okay. But if you're like me, you like your tasty meal every now and then. I have a friend who, after retirement, set aside every Thursday night as a "date night" with his wife. They go to their favorite restaurant and order their favorite food. During the week they watch what they eat but always with Thursday night in the back of their minds. I don't want to try and add to the already saturated subject of healthy living, I just want you to be mindful of it as part of your quest for a satisfying retirement.

12. KNOW WHAT MONEY CAN AND CAN'T BUY:

E. Stanley Jones told of being on a cruise ship. There was

A Funny Thing Happened on My Way to Work . . . I Retired

a rather corpulent couple on that cruise that seemed to live from one meal to the next. They were retired and obviously had plenty of money, but they seemed miserable. They were always angry with the table stewards for not giving them super-service. They seemed to be afraid they might starve between courses. They never read a book or paper. Their physical appetites seemed the one thing that mattered to them. They sat between meals and stared out, apparently waiting for the next meal.

One night Jones saw them sitting and staring blankly as usual, when the man suddenly noticed something. He went to the mantelpiece, picked up the vases, looked into them, and then returned to his wife with the news: "They're empty!" Jones came very near laughing. The man was right: "They're empty!" But it wasn't merely the vases! The souls and brains of both of these passengers were empty. They had a lot in their purses, said Jones, but nothing in their persons; and that was their punishment. They had security with boredom-no adventure.

This couple had expanded girths and narrowing horizons. I had a similar experience with a couple I invited to dinner. This couple is extremely wealthy but I chose to ask them out to dinner and pick up the ticket. First, the waiter was too *slow* to take their order. Next she was too *quick* to pick up their plates before they were finished. Finally, they wanted desert but were aghast that the waiter brought it *without* silverware. (It was a very busy night). When my wife and I got home and reflected on the evening, we realized how unhappy this affluent couple seemed to be.

Someone once wrote:

> *Money will buy a bed, but not sleep;*
> *Food, but not appetite;*
> *Books, but not knowledge;*
> *Medicine, but not health;*
> *Entertainment, but not happiness;*
> *A house, but not a home.*

Harvard Medical School Psychologist Steven Berglas wrote a book called *The Success Syndrome*. In his research he discovered that people who, in his word, "suffered" from 'success syndrome' were arrogant and had a sense of aloneness. He noted that affluence had a strange distancing effect. It created barriers.

You may or may not be an upcoming affluent retiree or one that is going to struggle to make ends meet after you leave your job. Either class of affluence can succumb to success syndrome. As I promised earlier, this book will deal with the practical as well as the psychological aspects of retirement. *It's okay to possess possessions, just don't let possessions possess you.*

CONCLUSION:

These are your twelve steps to Atlantis, or Paradise, or Nirvana, or . . . you get the idea. No amount of money or planning can create a fulfilling retirement if the priorities discussed in this chapter are out of balance. Priorities are what you make them.

That being said, you have taken a tremendously important step in this chapter by facing your fears and challenges head on and dealing with them. No matter what your attitude or outlook was on life before you started this book, I hope you have come to realize that change is possible when you have all the facts.

Case in point: A father was riding home on the subway with his three children. A passenger in the same car couldn't help but notice how loud and rambunctious the children were acting. The father seemed completely oblivious to their annoying behavior. The noise became so unbearable the passenger finally spoke to the dad. "Sir," he said, "are you completely unconcerned about your children's behavior?" The father seemed to snap out of a trance and looked at the passenger. "I'm sorry," he replied, "we are coming home from the hospital. Their mother just died and I don't think they know how to handle this terrible news." Needless to say, the passenger's attitude toward the children changed in an instant.

Having the right information can instantaneously change your perception and attitude toward a subject. Use what you have learned thus far to combat negative thinking and continue your journey through this book and ultimately to a joyful retirement.

"People will tell you that what you are doing is wrong. Then they will tell you that you are right, but what you are doing really isn't important. Finally they will admit that you are right and that what you are doing is very important; but after all, they knew it all the time."

-Jonas Salk
Inventor of the Salk Polio Vaccine

CHAPTER THREE

Let's Start Building the Ship

The United States, Japan and Russia each selected their best astronaut to participate in a joint two-year mission in space. At pre-launch briefing, the astronauts were told that they could take anything with them as long as it didn't weigh more than 125 pounds.

"My wife weighs 112 pounds," said the American. "I'd like to take her." The officials said that was fine. "I've always wanted to learn Greek," the Japanese astronaut said. "I'd like 125 pounds of books to teach myself the language." His request was also approved. "We'll be gone so long," spoke up the Russian, "that I want to take 125 pounds of the best Havana Cigars with me." His request was okayed, too. Two years later the astronauts returned to Earth. The American stepped out of the spaceship holding an infant in each arm. There was a roar of approval from the crowd. The Japanese astronaut stepped out and spoke to the world in flawless Greek. Again there was a roar of approval from the crowd. Then the Russian stepped out. His mouth was turned down and his teeth were clenched on the end of a cigar. He stepped up to the microphone and said sheepishly, "Would anybody have a match?"

Don't forget the small details! Someone once said the only stupid question is the one not asked. When facing retirement, it would be wise for you to ask a multitude of questions about every conceivable detail before making your final decision. "How will economic changes affect your income? Is there such a thing as political risk for your portfolio? What will you do if interest rates fall even lower or stay the way they are for

A Funny Thing Happened on My Way to Work . . . I Retired

several years?" These are good questions and, along with others, must be asked and answered, in order for you to step into a secure retirement.

I want you to understand that this chapter does not imply that by merely following these steps and others outlined in this book will guarantee a smooth retirement, *but* then again that is not my goal for you in the first place. My goal is to give you a structured vehicle that can weather the storms of economic uncertainty and empower you psychologically and financially so that you can remain afloat in rough seas. To put it in simple terms, I want to equip you to control the things you can control and survive the things you can't.

Dr. Norman Vincent Peale, in his book, *Stay Alive All Your Life,* tells about encountering a hurricane in the Atlantic. They managed to sail around danger, however. Afterwards, Dr. Peale and the captain were visiting. The captain said he had lived by the philosophy that if the sea is smooth, it will get rough, and if it is rough, it will get smooth. Then the captain added, *"But with a good ship you can always ride it out."* (Italics mine.)

I want to equip you with a good ship to ride out virtually any storm you come up against in your retirement experience.

Let me interject the motivation behind this desire of mine to help hardworking individuals like you reach retirement safely. My desire can be summed up in one passage: *"The gray head is a crown of glory,"* Proverbs 16:31a. I strongly believe that seniors are to be respected for their accomplishments in life and one way to do this is to help guide them (you) through the overwhelming task of retirement. Don't worry if your hair is not gray yet; it will be.

Let's get into the nuts and bolts of retirement planning and implementing. This chapter will require some extra effort on your part to accomplish what needs to be done. Grab a cup of coffee and set aside some quiet time. Plan to spend more than just a few minutes completing the exercises. In this chapter, we will explore:

- How to calculate your retirement income
- How to calculate your total living expenses
- How to keep up with the cost of living (Not the Jones)
- Ways to determine the future value of your retirement savings
- What effects inflation will have on your retirement dollars
- Investment recommendations: Including the nuts and bolts of bonds and CDs
- The power of compounding

You will be required to make several calculations in the upcoming pages. When you get going on the exercises you may start wondering if you're really capable of such requirements. You may be retiring from a job that didn't require much mathematical problem solving. So, is your brain capable?

Our brains are only two percent of our body weight, yet they receive twenty percent of the blood supply. The brain can store 100 trillion bits of information, but it only consumes enough power to light a 20-watt bulb. A fully formed human brain contains 100 billion neurons. A worm has twenty-three. Each neuron may have thousands of connections to other neurons; making a network that is far more complex than any computer network yet developed . . . I think you can handle the job.

* **NOTE:** Some of the calculators and tools offered in this book are located on various websites. Although the exercises contained herein can be done with a piece of paper and a simple desktop calculator, it would be helpful if the reader had access to a computer and the Internet. There are many advantages to knowing how to navigate the World Wide Web so if you are Internet challenged, I suggest you take a basic course on the subject. My 74-year-old mother-in-law did just that and now sends and receives email from her kids and buys merchandise online.

HOW TO CALCULATE YOUR RETIREMENT INCOME

Since income is the *lifeblood* of retirement, we must go to great lengths to discover what our income sources will be and what amounts we can expect. It is important to have the right knowledge before we delve into the unknown. Otherwise, we might not like the results.

A woman in the office approached the man standing behind a machine and asked, "How does this thing work?"

"Simple," said the man, taking the hefty report she was carrying and putting it through the document shredder.

"That's wonderful," she said, "how many copies does it make?"

We are well served to find the right information in order to avoid any accidental "shredding" of our dreams. What sources should you consider when calculating your retirement income?

According to the Social Security Administration, the majority of retirees receive their income from four primary sources:

1. Personal Savings and Investments Such as a Personal IRA or a Savings Account.
2. Earned Income or Wages Received from Active Employment. (In this case, active employment refers to full or part-time work after retirement).
3. Company Pension Benefits.
4. Social Security Income.

Since the foundation of any retirement is the financial ability to stay retired, it behooves us to have a firm knowledge of our income sources and amounts.

During the construction of the Titanic, an estimated 3 million rivets were hammered into her hull. Can you imagine how tedious a task this was? Yet, every tiny rivet served a purpose. What I am about to ask you to do will seem tedious and cumbersome, but it *will* serve you well when the waters of uncertainty get rough, so please, don't cut corners here.

I have tried to make this section of the book as user-friendly as possible. Just take a common-sense approach to each task. What we are trying to determine here is the solvency of your income as it relates to your expenses. I also want to get you thinking about income and expenses you might not have otherwise considered.

Is your coffee cup full? Below is a chart to help you gather your income information. Take extra time to complete this exercise. Research and gather all the paperwork you need to accurately fill out each section. It will be an eye-opener for you now *and* the results will be used later in the book and ultimately in retirement. This chapter might take several hours to complete. I suggest you break up your research and study times into small segments. You don't have to complete this chapter before going on to the next. Each chapter is self-contained and is not a prerequisite to the next one.

Below the chart is the web address for calculating your Social Security income. I have also posted the link on my website at www.stevekiefer.com. Just select the "Calculators" button. When you are at the site, simply enter your date of birth, your gross income from last year and hit the submit button. It's that easy. If you are a few months away from retirement, be sure to select the "today's dollars" option. If retirement is a few years down the road, select the "future dollars."

For any employment related income source, consult your plan administrator at work. They can give you the best idea regarding your pension and insurance coverage. For the remainder of your income sources required in the upcoming calculations, talk to your financial advisor or banker. They should be able to help you determine what you can expect from your personal investments. A word of caution here; explain to your advisor(s) that you are not looking for the maximum withdrawal amount as this can put unnecessary pressure on your holdings. Instead, ask them to quote a "reasonable" stream of income that you won't likely outlive. I want you to determine whether you will have enough income to meet financial needs or not. This may sound overly simplistic, but it can mean the difference between a retirement of comfort and one of total stress.

Is the coffee ready?

Steve Kiefer

(Exercise One)
CALCULATE YOUR RETIREMENT INCOME

CATEGORY	SOURCE	MONTHLY $	ANNUAL $
Government and Social Security Income	Social Security On <u>Your</u> Earnings*		
	Social Security On <u>Spouseís</u> Earnings		
	Veteran Benefits		
	TOTAL	$	$
Employer	Company Pension		
	Keogh		
	Profit Sharing		
	Other		
	TOTAL	$	$
Personal Savings	IRA		
	Interest from Savings		
	Money Market		
	Interest from CDs		
	Stock Dividends		
	Bond Interest		
	Mutual Fund Dividends		
	Systematic Liquidation		
	Variable Annuities		
	Fixed Annuities		
	TOTAL	$	$
Real Estate/ Business	Rental Income		
	Royalties		
	Partnerships		
	Other		
	TOTAL	$	$
Wages	Part or Full Time Work		
	Hobbies		
	Commissions		
	Residuals		
	Other		
GRAND TOTAL	$		$

*As I mentioned, it will take some work to get this done. To determine your projected Social Security income on you and/or your spouse's earnings, go to: www.ssa.gov/OACT/quickcalc/calculator.html or go to the chapter on Social Security to find out how to calculate this figure.

Keep the monthly and annual totals handy for another exercise coming up later in the book.

HOW TO CALCULATE YOUR TOTAL LIVING EXPENSES

Calculating income is a pleasant task compared to the chore of adding up the bills. Consider this a necessary evil that we need to accomplish to continue our trek. This might get a little depressing so take it slow. Later I will be asking you to list the balances that are due on your liabilities, but here I am just looking for your actual expenses.

Example: You have a car with a $10,000 balance and the payments are $375 per month, I want you to list the $375 here. We will list the $10,000 balance in the chapter on net worth.

A certain man made an application for a position and was being interviewed by the personnel manager. He was told that the company had group insurance for their employees but that each employee paid for his own coverage. The cost would be deducted from the first paycheck of each month. The man looked very disappointed. Noting his disappointment, the interview asked him if that presented a problem.

"At my last place of employment, the company paid for everything," he said. "They paid for our life insurance, dental insurance, health insurance, three weeks paid vacation, a Christmas bonus, and unlimited sick leave."

"I can't imagine why you would leave such a generous employer," the personnel man said.

After a moment of silence the man said sheepishly, "They went bankrupt."

Before we commit to "extras" in retirement, we need to find out what the basics are costing us so we don't "bankrupt" our future.

As with the income chart, I have included a table to help you calculate all of your liabilities. The more time you spend on this exercise the less likely an unpleasant surprise will rear its ugly head after retirement has begun. For this very reason, I have purposely created this exercise in *great* detail. Bear with me. (Remember, I am looking for actual monthly expenses here. Don't put any balances due in this section.)

One main difference in this table as opposed to the one you just completed is the monthly column. Due to the extra calculations required to factor in inflation, I did not have room to include it here. As a result, I condensed it to one calculation and moved it to the page following the chart. I want a dual-purpose accomplished here. First, I want you to determine your current level of expenses, and second, I want you to calculate the projected inflation costs that will come every year. I suggest that you complete these exercises at least once every year, or when a major financial event occurs, in order to keep your balance sheet current. As time goes on you will pay off old debts and incur new ones. I will ask the same from you when you start calculating your net worth.

(In this exercise, inflation is estimated at 4%, which is based on the Bureau of Labor Statistics' Consumer Price Index average inflation rate for a 50-year period.)

A Funny Thing Happened on My Way to Work . . . I Retired

(Exercise Two)
CALCULATE YOUR TOTAL LIABILITIES

Retirement Costs			
Expense Item	Last Year's Annual Cost X 4%* (A) Cost (B) Increase	Add A to B	Projected Future Expense
House Payment Example:	$5,500 X .04 = 220	5,500 + 220 =	$5,720
Housing: Mortgage Payment	X .04	+ =	
Property Taxes	X .04	+ =	
Natural Gas	X .04	+ =	
Electric	X .04	+ =	
Water/sewer/garbage	X .04	+ =	
Phone/Cell Bill	X .04	+ =	
House Cleaning	X .04	+ =	
Repair/Yard work	X .04	+ =	
Floor and Window	X .04	+ =	
Insurance: Home	X .04	+ =	
Health	X .04	+ =	
Life	X .04	+ =	
Auto	X .04	+ =	
Vacation/other	X .04	+ =	
		Sub Total I	

*The 4% increase is to account for inflation.

Expense Item (Continued)	Last Year's Annual Cost X 4% (A) Cost / (B) Increase	Add A to B	Projected Future Expense
Transportation: Annual Car Payment	X .04	+ =	
Oil/Tires	X .04	+ =	
Gasoline (ouch)	X .04	+ =	
Repair	X .04	+ =	
Airline/Bus/Taxi	X .04	+ =	
License/Registration	X .04	+ =	
Clothing: Household clothing	X .04	+ =	
Dry Cleaning	X .04	+ =	
Floor and Window	X .04	+ =	
Food Entertainment Groceries	X .04	+ =	
Eating out	X .04	+ =	
Vacation	X .04	+ =	
Movies/Sports	X .04	+ =	
Cable/Computer	X .04	+ =	
Memberships/Dues	X .04	+ =	
Healthcare: Medications/Drugs	X .04	+ =	
Co-pay Dr/Dentist	X .04	+ =	
Glasses/Hearing Aids	X .04	+ =	
Donations: Church	X .04	+ =	
Charities	X .04	+ =	
Other:	X .04	+ =	
		Sub Total II	

Sub Total I _____
Sub Total II _____
GRAND TOTAL _____

You have just stepped out from the majority into the minority by completing this exercise. Few workers have a good idea of how much it takes to fund a comfortable retirement nor given thought to key retirement issues. Many who save don't take advantage of available vehicles to prepare for retirement.

Did you know that the *majority* of American workers have not tried to calculate how much they will need to save for retirement? Only 42 percent of workers report they and/or their spouse have tried to calculate how much money they will need to save by the time they retire so that they can live comfortably in retirement. *Source: Employee Benefits Research Institute, American Savings Education Council, and Mathew Greeenwald & Associates, Inc., 1994–2004 Retirement Confidence Surveys.*

Of the pre-retirees who did use a retirement savings calculator, over 40 percent reported that they made changes to their retirement planning as a result of the calculations.

I read a financial planner's opinion of why the rich get richer and the poor get poorer. Simply put, he said the poor get poorer because they continue to do the things that made them poor in the first place. You've heard the definition of insanity: Doing the same things over and over yet expecting different results. You *have* to stretch yourself to attain your goals. Completing this book with all of the exercises in it will allow you to make a giant step toward those goals. Don't give up!

Now for an easy one: Take the grand total of your *expenses* and divide it by 12.

Grand Total_____ ÷ 12 = _____
                                                Monthly Expense

You should now have an average monthly total of your

income as well as a monthly total of your projected expenses. Next, we need to decide which one is greater. Following are two examples of surplus and deficit.

Monthly Surplus
Example I: *$2,356* - *$2,003* = *$353*
            Income   Expense   Surplus

In this example you would have a monthly surplus of $353 over and above your normal expenses. This is a good sign that your plan is working.

Monthly Deficit
Example II: *$2,741* - *$2,138* = *($603)*
            Expense Income   Deficit

In this example we see a need to make some adjustments. We either need to increase our monthly income sources by $603 or reduce our monthly payments by the same amount. Don't panic if this is the case. Remember, these numbers are projections that serve to give us a point of reference to work from. A point of reference can be a powerful ally. Adm. Richard E. Byrd was the first man to over-winter alone in Antarctica, manning the Bolling Advance Weather Base on the Ross Ice Barrier for four and a half months in 1934. But he very nearly perished for the distinction.

Once during a brief exploration from his base, Admiral Byrd was caught in a sudden blizzard. He had no idea which way camp was and he dared not strike out in a direction that might lead him away from the relative safety of his tent.

He came up with a plan. He took the pole that he used to probe for hidden crevasses and stuck it in the snow. Next, he took off his brightly colored scarf and tied it to the top of the pole. He began to walk in a circle around the pole in search of camp. After completing a circle, he would enlarge his search always keeping his eyes on his point of reference. After several attempts, he found his tent and was saved. *Had he not maintained a point of reference to keep going back to, he would have been lost forever.*

The figures from the exercises above are just our point of reference. We will use them to find our way back to camp i.e. a comfortable retirement.

Based on the two examples above, let's figure your point of reference.

Take the smallest of your expense and income grand totals and subtract it from the largest.

$$\underset{\text{Largest Total}}{\underline{\hspace{2cm}}} - \underset{\text{Smallest Total}}{\underline{\hspace{2cm}}} = \underset{\text{Surplus (Deficit)}}{\underline{\hspace{2cm}}}$$

Again, let me stress it is very important to repeat this exercise at least once a year as more accurate data is made available. Doing this exercise on an annual basis will help you keep tabs on inflation and income. Don't be surprised to find the expense total to be lower than you first estimated due to the fact that the elimination of work expenses can dramatically decrease your monthly outflow. Some analysts estimate that cost reductions can be as much as 30% due to removal of employment expenses from the budget. For now though we will keep them in the calculations to act as a buffer.

An ideal time of year to do this exercise is during tax season. I can hear you lamenting, "I'm swamped at tax time just trying to get all of my files together before April 15!" This exercise will prove to be an asset to your tax calculations rather than a distraction. You basically do the work anyway, so take advantage of the situation and update your numbers while you are doing taxes. You might even find a deduction or two that you would have missed otherwise.

Back to your final figure; if you find there is a deficit or a break-even result from the exercise above, it is imperative that you find a way to either increase income via part-time work, etc., or decrease expenses. A good buffer should be a 20% surplus each month.

Example: Expense-$1,600 / Income-$2,000 = $400 surplus (20%)

If you are faced with a large expense due to illness, accident, etc., think about alternate ways to meet the debt other than cashing in securities. If you have a "rainy day" lump sum, good for you. If, however, you use the majority of your holdings to generate your retirement income, consider various loans. Home equity loans are cheap and easy to get. Borrowing against some of your holdings via a margin loan can be a good source for emergency cash. Talk to your financial professional about your options.

HOW TO KEEP UP WITH THE COST OF LIVING

Q: How much will my income need to increase to keep up with the cost of living?

According to the Consumer Price Index, the cost of living has fluctuated, but has averaged between 4% and 5% per year over the past 20 years. As a rule of thumb, I encourage my clients to estimate a 5% withdrawal for income expenses and leave the remainder gain (provided there is a gain in their portfolio) to outpace or at least keep up with inflation. In some cases a 7% withdrawal is appropriate but keep in mind that these figures are only examples. There are many factors that both my clients and I consider before a withdrawal cap is set.

DETERMINE THE FUTURE VALUE OF YOUR RETIREMENT SAVINGS

THIS SECTION IS ONLY FOR PEOPLE WHO HAVE AT LEAST FIVE YEARS OR MORE UNTIL RETIREMENT. If you are already 65, you can skip to the next topic "What effect

A Funny Thing Happened on My Way to Work . . . I Retired

inflation has on your retirement dollars" or you can alert someone you know about the power of time investing.

Let's begin with a calculation of your future earnings. I've inserted a chart that will allow you to calculate what your nest egg will be worth when you turn 65. I am assuming, of course, that you are under the age of 65 and possibly still saving for the final event. If you are 65 or older, be sure to check out the "How long will my money last" chart. It will be an eye-opener.

Determine your future value. Assume you will put back **$250** per month into a retirement account. If you do this faithfully every month until age 65, you can see what your total savings will be at that time. A good rule of thumb is to estimate an average return of between 7 and 9%.

Age	Total amount Invested to 65	4%	7%	9%	12%
25	$120,000	$296,475	$660,031	$1,179,108	$2,970,605
30	$105,000	$229,194	$452,890	$740,962	$1,623817
35	$90,000	$174,091	$306,772	$461,119	$882,478 *
40	$75,000	$128,961	$203,699	$282,383	$474,409
45	$60,000	$91,999	$130,991	$168,224	$249,787
50	$45,000	$61,728	$79,703	$95,311	$126,144
55	$30,000	$36,935	$43,524	$48,741	$58,085
60	$15,000	$16,630	$18,003	$18,997	$20,622

This chart vividly elucidates the time value of money. The longer you have to save, the more of a bundle you will have at retirement age.

*Example. You are a 35 year old business owner who has decided to start saving for retirement. You put in $250 a month beginning on your 35th birthday. Since you are young, you are a little aggressive and it pays off. You see an average annual return on your money of 12%. At age 65 you will have a handsome nest egg valued at $882,478. Not bad. (The assumption in the above chart is that this money has grown tax-deferred, thus the figures are all pre-tax amounts).

Steve Kiefer

WHAT EFFECT INFLATION HAS ON YOUR RETIREMENT DOLLARS

Q: What Has Inflation Looked Like Over the Past Twenty Years?

As I discussed earlier in chapter one, inflation is a real risk to anyone's portfolio. The figures I used in diagram one were based on only a 4% inflation rate. Let's look at some actual historical figures to further illustrate the impact of inflation.

Let's assume you retired in 1980 and you needed a retirement income of $4,000 per month. Just five short years later, what cost $4,000 in 1980 would now cost $5,724.27 in 1985. That means you would need to bring in an additional $1,724.27 to buy the same goods and services in 1985 that you consumed in 1980. Five years later (1990) the same goods would now cost $6,830.08. Twenty years into your retirement, what used to cost $4,000 in 1980 would now cost $9,147.49 in the year 2000 according to the Consumer Price Index from 1980-2000. In other words, you would need to *more than double* your income just to keep the same purchasing power you enjoyed twenty years earlier. Wow! (More on this subject in Chapter four).

I can almost see the cold chill running down your spine. Don't panic! Before you succumb to the fear of having to work until you are 143 years old, I have some good news.

Since 1940, the average return of the largest companies, the S&P 500 index, is around 13%. Notice I said *average*. From 1940 until 2002 the S&P had 47 up years out of 63. In that same time, the S&P decreased in value 16 years. In other words, about three out of four years the market rises. So once again, the *average* trend of the market is a gain of 13% a year.

Previously, I mentioned how I encourage many of my clients to cap their withdrawal rate as close to 5% as possible. The reason should be obvious to you now. If we only attain an average return of say 11% instead of the historical 13%, we not only keep up with inflation by withdrawing only 5%, but we actually grow the value of the portfolio faster than inflation can eat it away resulting in a gain. The result? Not only does this plan allow my clients to give themselves a raise each year (I recommend every five years if possible), it also causes the balance of the account to increase in value, offering a more lucrative inheritance for the heirs of the retiree. (More on the subject of inflation later.)

INVESTMENT RECOMMENDATIONS

Q: What kind of investments do you recommend for retirees?

I will try to be as specific as possible here but I want you to realize that every retiree is different with unique financial and retirement needs.

As a rule, investments should be based on an individuals need for growth and income as well as safety of principal and liquidity.

Rather than approach this section by naming specific securities, I want to give you an outline to use when putting together your investment portfolio. This approach follows the wise saying, "Give me a fish and I'll eat for a day; *teach* me to fish and I'll eat for a lifetime." Let's begin with time. Generally speaking, most retirees have the need for three time horizons: Short-term investments, intermediate investments, and long-term investments.

1. Short-term investments. 1 to 3 years:

When dealing with short-term investments, I generally keep my clients in financial instruments such as Cash, Money Market Funds, CDs and T Bills. Some short-term bonds with a maturity date of five years or less can fit into this category as well.*

* **A NOTE ABOUT BONDS**
    ♦ MATURITIY DATES:
    Be sure not to confuse a bond's maturity date with its call

date. A maturity date is the day, month, and year the bond will end its existence resulting in the bond owner receiving his or her initial investment back at par. (Par is equal to $1,000 per bond). A CALL date is simply a date when the issuer of the bond has the *option* to call the bond back and return the investor's money. The call date does not guarantee a return of principal on that day. This can greatly affect your actual interest earned on the bond; therefore I use two calculations to refer to the interest earned on a bond:

A: The yield to maturity

B: The yield to worst or the yield to call

Example: You purchase a GMAC bond that matures in thirteen years. It has a coupon rate of 7% interest. The cost of the bond is $1018.28 per bond. It is callable in one month at par ($1000). Since you paid a premium (amount above par) for the bond you won't realize the full 7% interest no matter how long you hold it. If the bond is kept until maturity, you will receive an average of 6.769% per year for the entire thirteen years. Not bad.

However, if the bond is called back in one month the average return drops to 3.263% per year and you will only receive one month's worth of it.

Sometimes the yield to call and the yield to maturity are the same but as we have seen in this illustration they can be vastly different. Be mindful of this discrepancy when purchasing a bond of any length.

♦ BOND VALUES AND INTEREST RATES

Speaking of length, there is one other important characteristic about bonds that you need to know. (People that are accustomed to purchasing CDs will find bonds offer a rude awakening if they don't know what's coming. Remember, WACK!)

Bond values can fluctuate drastically depending on the rise or fall of interest rates. We are coming out of an interest rate recession where rates have reached 40-year lows. How will your

A Funny Thing Happened on My Way to Work . . . I Retired

bonds be affected when rates go up? Let's go to the playground to find out.

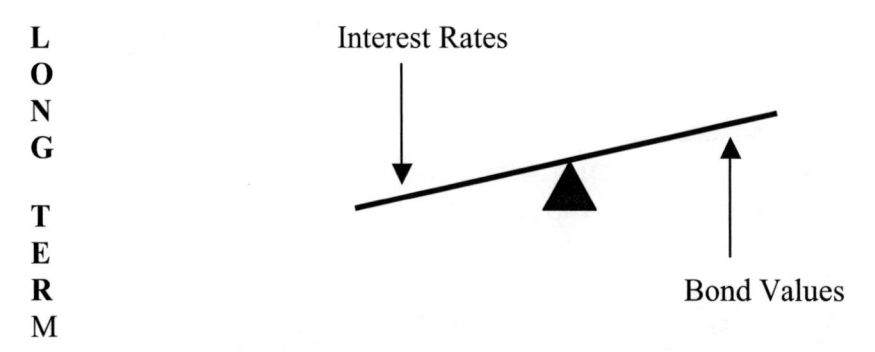

L
O
N
G

T
E
R
M

Interest Rates

Bond Values

As you can see from our teeter-totter illustration, bond values move in direct contrast to interest rates. Example: Joe buys ten bonds at par (10 X $1,000 = $10,000). The bonds are yielding 6% and will mature in 25 years.

a. *If Interest Rates Drop*

If interest rates go down, the value of Joe's bonds will go up as shown in the illustration above. The reason: the better the interest rate on a bond is, the more valuable it is in the market. If the highest bonds available are only paying 5% and you own this one paying 6%, people will pay you more (AKA a premium) so they can get a better interest rate than the market will bear. So the bonds that Joe paid $10,000 for may be selling for $11,000. He can choose to keep them or sell them for a profit. (One important fact to remember with bonds is the interest is paid on the *par value* of the bond never on the *market value*. The market value can go up or down as I am describing in this section, but the holder of the bonds in this example will continue to receive $600 per year in interest: $10,000 (Par Value) X 6%(Interest Rate) = $600). Don't multiply the market value (in this case $11,000) by 6%. The only way this would change is if the bond went into default. Hence, watch out for bonds below investment grade, or bonds better known as "Junk Bonds."

The risk is this: if you buy a long term bond (in the example above it was 25 years) a million things can happen to you during the life of the bond. If you **need** to sell a portion to pay for an emergency, you might get back more, less, or the same amount you originally put in.

I am a big believer in short-term bonds right now due to the fact that interest rates are most likely going to go up. At the writing of this book the feds have raised short-term rates twice. Let's look at our teeter-totter again and see what happens to short term bonds (Maturities from three to five years).

b. *If Interest Rates Rise*

If interest rates start to go up, the value of the bonds will drop. For example, interest on available bonds has gone up to the point where investors can purchase them at par and receive 7% return. Now, what has happened to Joe's bonds? They are less attractive. Who wants to buy bonds paying 6% when for the same price they can buy bonds paying 7%? Thus the value of Joe's bonds go down. Now they might be worth $9,000 (AKA a discount). Again, the interest Joe will receive is still $600 because the 6% is paid on the *par value* not the *market value*. (Is it starting to sink in?)

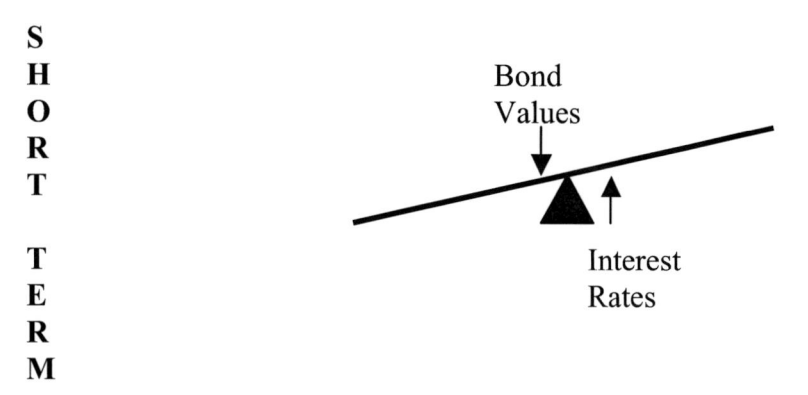

S
H
O
R
T

                  Bond
                  Values

T
E   Interest
R   Rates
M

As you can see from this illustration, the closer we move toward the center, the less volatility there is with the bond val-

A Funny Thing Happened on My Way to Work . . . I Retired

ues. Short-term bonds react this way. A five-year bond will *drop* much less in value when interest rates rise than will a 25-year bond. Consequently, a five-year bond will *rise* much less in value when interest rates go down than will a 25-year bond.

2. INTERMEDIATE INVESTMENTS. 3 TO 10 YEARS:

In the intermediate sector I tend to broaden my client's holding into securities like fixed annuities, municipal bonds, government bonds, and multi-step CDs.*

*Multi-step CDs are callable CDs that offer an increase in interest the longer the instrument is held. Example: One of my clients, Mrs. I. M. Frugal, buys a five-year CD from me that pays 4% interest the first year. Since this is a multi-step CD, and assuming it will not be called back, (see my explanation on bond calls above) the interest it pays will go up.

FIVE-YEAR MULTI-STEP CD

Year	Interest Rate
1	4%
2	4.5%
3	5%
4	6%
5	7%

As you can see by this chart, if Mrs. Frugal keeps the CD for the full five years, she will receive seven percent during the final year of ownership. A word of caution here: be sure to have your broker give you the *ROR or real rate of return* of interest that the callable CD will pay if held to maturity. In the illustration above, Mrs. Frugal will receive a total average of 5.3% interest per year if she holds the CD for the entire five years. (4 + 4.5 + 5 + 6 + 7 = 26.5 divided by 5 = 5.3% average interest per year). This is probably confusing but it is important that you know what you are getting when you purchase any type of security.

Let me say a word about CDs in general here. CDs have a place in most portfolios but be careful, they usually aren't the best choice when it comes to *growing* your money. They are better suited for use as cash-equivalent instruments and for liquidity.

Let me illustrate. The following chart shows the ***actual*** performance of CDs over the past ten years. All data shown is compiled from the ***Federal Reserve Bank*** website and all inflation data is sourced from the ***Bureau of Labor Statistics.*** For the after-tax performance, we have assumed a 28% income tax rate.

> The following chart shows the *actual* performance of CDs over the past ten years. All data shown is compiled from the **Federal Reserve Bank** website and all inflation data is sourced from the **Bureau of Labor Statistics.** For the after-tax performance, we have assumed a 28% income tax rate.

Year	CD Rate	After Tax	Inflation	Real ROR*
1993	3.28	2.36	2.75	-0.39
1994	4.96	3.57	2.68	0.89
1995	5.98	4.31	2.54	1.77
1996	5.47	3.94	3.32	0.62
1997	5.73	4.13	1.70	2.43
1998	5.44	3.926	1.61	2.31
1999	5.46	3.93	2.69	1.24
2000	6.59	4.74	3.39	1.35
2001	3.66	2.64	1.60	1.04
2002	1.81	1.30	2.40	-1.10
AVE				1.02

*REAL RATE OF RETURN

As you can see from this chart, ten one-year CDs returned an average 1.02 percent *after* taxes and inflation. Let me introduce a simple formula know as the "Rule of 72." Rule 72 is a simple equation used to determine how many years it will take your money to double. It looks like this: 72 divided by (Interest Rate) = Number of years to double your money.

Example: You hold an investment that is paying 8% per year in interest. Using our formula: 72/8 = **9**, we discover that it will take nine years for our money to double at a compounded rate of eight percent per year.

Now, let's put our CD rate to the same test. Remember that our CDs are paying, on average, 1.02 percent per year. 72/1.02 = 70.59. At this rate of interest it will take 70 and one half years to double our money if we use one-year CDs for growth. Don't make the mistake of using a teaspoon to bail out a sinking ship. Get the right instrument for the right task.

3. LONG-TERM INSTRUMENTS. 10 TO 25 YEARS AND BEYOND:

Now we're getting into the good stuff. Equity and real estate positions are good vehicles to reach long-term growth. Variable annuities offer an excellent source of growth with various "layers" of protection for the investor. Equity mutual funds, equity unit trusts, and common stocks are other great options for growth as well.

When dealing with common stocks, I prefer to spread my client's holdings over several different sectors. Generally, it is wise to have holdings in at least five sectors to be properly diversified in individual stocks. I'm not saying you should never own an individual stock by itself. It is ok to keep small portions of your portfolio in one or two stocks, but when the percentages start to climb, it is time to diversity.

I'm sure you've heard someone say they never made any money in the stock market while others say they lost money in equities. Although the reasons for these reactions can be numerous, I basically see it as a "herd" mentality. A herd mentality occurs when investors follow the masses in their investment practices. They buy when everyone is buying and sell when everyone is selling. They might buy when good news is abundant and sell when times seem their bleakest. I find it amusing when people tell me they don't want to invest in the stock market right now because it's too volatile. Excuse me, but has there ever been a day when the market wasn't volatile? That's like saying, "I don't want to go swimming today because the water is too wet." It would be easier to sit in your own lap than to pick a non-volatile day in the stock market.

The old saying of "buy low and sell high" is in direct opposition to the "herd" mentality. This is much easier said than done. Repeatedly, the best time to buy has been when people are selling. Consequently, the best time to sell has been when (you are a smart one aren't you) people are buying. I have a real grenade on my desk (disarmed I think). When a client sees their equity holdings drop I tell them this; If you feel like throwing a grenade through my window, be sure to attach a check to it, because that is precisely when you need to be buying. Don't misunderstand what I am saying here. I am not advocating that a good approach to investing is timing the market. On the contrary, I believe that time *in* the market is far more valuable than trying to follow the latest trends. In addition, there are no guarantees with stock ownership, yet, in spite of the negative reasons not to be in the market, many patient investors have enjoyed very attractive returns over 10–20 year holding periods. Since most retirees have at least 10 to 20 years to leave a *portion* of their money invested (and they really should), stocks and equity mutual funds are an excellent investment vehicle for a select amount of their retirement dollars

THE POWER OF COMPOUNDING:

Compounding, simply put, is when you earn interest on your principle then interest on the interest. Example: You have $50 and it earns 10% or $5. Now you have $55 and it earns 10% but the gain is now $5.50 because of compounding. You made

A Funny Thing Happened on My Way to Work . . . I Retired

10% on the initial investment of $50 and 10% on the interest it earned in the previous year.

The best strategy for saving is called "triple compounding." Triple compounding is when you earn:

1. Interest on principal
2. Interest on interest
3. Interest on deferred taxes

When you put money into a tax-deferred investment, you receive triple compounding. You don't have to pay income tax on your gains until you pull the money out from under the tax-deferred umbrella. This "umbrella" might be an IRA, or an annuity or some other tax-sheltered account. This technique allows you to pay taxes on gains when *you* want to. It puts you in control. While the tax money remains in a tax-sheltered environment, it can earn interest for you. Below is a chart showing what $100,000 can grow to utilizing the triple compounding method:

Guarantee Period	Guaranteed Rate*	What Will grow to $100,000²	What $100,000 will grow to²
10 Year	**5.25%**	**$59,950**	**$166,810**
9 Year	5.00%	$64,462	$155,133
8 Year	4.80%	$68,725	$145,509
7 Year	4.55%	$73,238	$136,543
6 Year	4.25%	$77,902	$128,368
5 Year	4.00%	$82,194	$121,665

As you can see from this example, $100,000 invested in a five year, tax-deferred account paying 4%, will grow to $121,665 due to triple compounding. Your actual rate of return (ROR) will be 4.33% per year or 21.665% for the full five years equaling a total gain of $21,665.

If, on the other hand, your money is in taxable (nontax deferred) account, you will be forced to pay taxes on the gains at the end of each year. If you were in the 30% tax bracket during this five year period, your $100,000 would only grow to $114,806 with $14,806 being your total gain after taxes. So, instead of getting a 4.33% rate of return per year, your ROR would drop to 2.96% for a total of 14.8% for the full five-year term. With tax-deferred triple compounding, however, you will gain a positive difference of $6,859.

On the ten-year investment instead of earning 43.5%, the percentage jumps to 66.81% or a difference of $23,347. Wow! The third tier of compounding earned you an extra $23,347 on your total return. Even if you have to pay tax from the top bracket of 40% you still walk away with an additional $14,008.

Let's go out a little further.

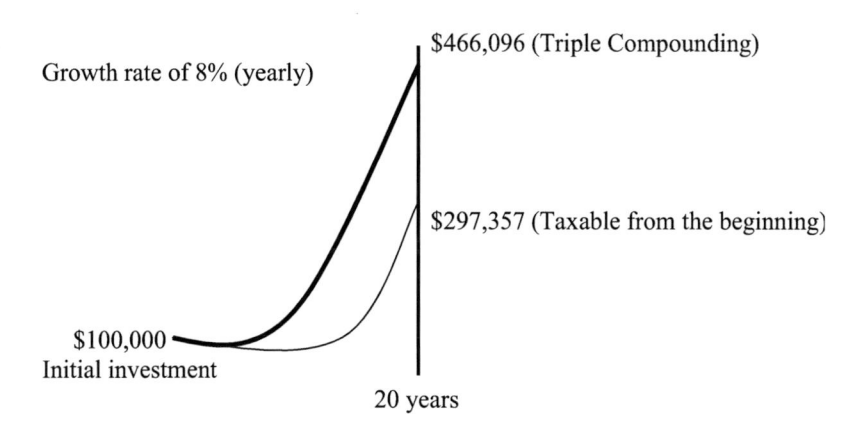

Growth rate of 8% (yearly)

$466,096 (Triple Compounding)

$297,357 (Taxable from the beginning)

$100,000
Initial investment

20 years

Again, if you are in the 40% tax bracket, you would still come out way ahead. $466,096 - $297,357 = $168,739 (The gross amount generated by the third tier of compounding.)

$168,739 X 40% = $67,496 in taxes due

$168,739 - $67,496 = $**101,243** in after tax profit above the original return of $297,357.

Deferring taxes as long as you can is a great way to grow and sustain your investment dollars. In many cases, the tax bracket of a retiree will go down after leaving the workforce, but I wanted you to see the worst-case scenario figures in my example.

CONCLUSION:

If the discussion about callable bonds, CDs, and triple compounding has *thoroughly* confused you I have accomplished one of my goals. I simply want you to understand the complexity of investing and the importance of seeking professional help before any investments are made. If you have any questions, contact your local financial advisor or look for a seminar to go to. Teaching seminars are becoming more popular everyday so ask around.

Happiness is having your priorities in order.

-Anonymous

CHAPTER FOUR

WHAT MAKES YOU SEASICK

DETERMINING YOUR RISK TOLERANCE

One foggy night the captain of a large ship saw what appeared to be another ship's running lights approaching in the distance. The other ship was evidently on a course that would result in a head-on collision. The captain quickly signaled to the approaching ship, "Please change your course 10 degrees west."

The reply returned back, blinking through the fog: "You change your course 10 degrees east." The Captain became furious and shot a message back to the other ship, "I'm a sea captain with thirty-five years experience. You change your course 10 degrees west!" Without waiting, the signal flashed back, "I'm a seaman fourth class. You change your course 10 degrees east!" Enraged and incensed, the captain knew that he was heading for a terrible head on crash. He blazed a last message to the fast approaching ship: "I'm a 50,000 ton freighter. You change your course 10 degrees west!" The simple message winked back, "I'm a **lighthouse**! You change . . ."

Understanding your tolerance for investment risk relative to your investment return expectations is an important step in designing a retirement portfolio. Some investors, like our dear freighter captain, think they're headed for a simple problem, which they think they can handle when, in reality, they are heading for the rocks. On the other hand, some think they are headed for the rocks when in reality what they see is only their

109

A Funny Thing Happened on My Way to Work . . . I Retired

reflection. This chapter will help you determine which type of investor you are when it comes to risk tolerance. It will also offer several suggestions that you can use *regardless* of your risk tolerance.

I've listed some questions that will help you develop a more accurate financial picture of your life and will help give you a good idea of your possible income during retirement. The answers you select will indicate your comfort level with investment risk and your ability to withstand it. This exercise will also show you how prepared you are to finance your retirement. Whatever you do, don't skip this part!

In this chapter you will discover:

- Your Level of Investment Experience
    - Interest Rate
    - Inflation
    - Taxes
    - What amount of return you will need to beat these icebergs
- Your Level of Risk Tolerance
    - Risk Category
- Recommended Portfolio Mixes
- Five Ways to Ease Taxes in Retirement

I. YOUR LEVEL OF INVESTMENT EXPERIENCE

To establish your risk tolerance, we must begin with your investment experience. The more you know and understand an investment the more comfortable you will be utilizing it. (Remember my swimming hole experience). Put a check mark in the box that best describes your knowledge of that particular security:

Experience Level	Stocks	Bonds	Mutual Funds	Annuities	Options
Low 0 to 2 yrs					
Moderate 2 to 5 yrs					
Extensive 5+ yrs					

If you scored consistently low on most or all of the categories, it simply means you have some homework to do on various investments. Don't let fear of the unknown cost you income potential. You've already increased your knowledge of bonds and callable CDs in previous chapters. (If you feel like the bond and CD information didn't sink in the first time, read it again in a few days. It will begin to make sense soon).

There is a true story about a woman who was about to be evicted by her landlord for falling too far behind in her rent. She shared her plight with her pastor one Sunday morning after the service. After she left the church, the pastor made a few calls and raised the funds necessary to bring the woman's rent up to date. He went to pick up the pledges and quickly drove to the woman's apartment. Expectantly, he knocked on the door, excited about the gift in his hand. There was no answer. He knocked again a little louder this time. Still there was no answer. After several more attempts, the pastor left disappointed. He did not see the woman for several days, then one afternoon he ran into her while he was conducting a service at the homeless shelter. He told the woman about the money he raised and how he tried to reach her with the funds. Sheepishly, the woman confessed, "When you came and knocked on my door that day, I thought you were the landlord coming to collect the rent. I was afraid he might have come to throw me out so I didn't answer the door. If only I had known it was you."

So many people have discovered the painful truth that fear can cost them dearly. Many who are dependent on the cur-

A Funny Thing Happened on My Way to Work . . . I Retired

rent interest rates for their financial survival, find themselves frozen from fear at the thought of losing their principal. As a result, they seek the pseudo-shelter of bank CDs and never venture past their FDIC insured comfort blanket. Look at the chart below to see what CD rates are up against when taxes and inflation are factored in.

BREAK-EVEN CHART FOR U.S.

STATE	STATE TAX*	BREAK-EVEN AMOUNT	STATE	STATE TAX*	BREAK-EVEN AMOUNT
Alabama	5.00%	5.71%	Nebraska	6.84%	5.86%
Alaska	0.00%	5.33%	Nevada	0.00%	5.33%
Arizona	5.04%	5.71%	New Hampshire	5.00%**	5.71%
Arkansas	6.50%	5.83%	New Jersey	6.37%	5.82%
California	9.30%	6.08%	New Mexico	8.20%	5.98%
Colorado	4.63%	5.68%	New York	6.85%	5.86%
Connecticut	4.50%	5.67%	North Carolina	8.25%	5.99%
Delaware	5.95%	5.79%	North Dakota	5.54%	5.75%
District of Columbia	8.70%	6.03%	Ohio	7.50%	5.92%
Florida	0.00%	5.33%	Oklahoma	7.00%	5.88%
Georgia	6.00%	5.79%	Oregon	9.00%	6.06%
Hawaii	8.25%	5.99%	Pennsylvania	2.80%	5.54%
Idaho	7.80%	5.95%	Rhode Island	25% of Fed	5.81%
Illinois	3.00%	5.55%	South Carolina	7.00%	5.88%
Indiana	3.40%	5.58%	South Dakota	0.00%	5.33%
Iowa	8.98%	6.05%	Tennessee	6.00%**	5.79%
Kansas	6.45%	5.83%	Texas	0.00%	5.33%
Kentucky	6.00%	5.79%	Utah	7.00%	5.88%
Louisiana	6.00%	5.79%	Vermont	9.50%	6.01%
Main	8.50%	6.01%	Virginia	5.75%	5.77%
Maryland	4.75%	5.69%	Washington	0.00%	5.33%
Massachusetts	5.00%	5.71%	West Virginia	6.50%	5.83%
Michigan	4.00%	5.63%	Wisconsin	6.75%	5.86%
Minnesota	7.85%	5.95%	Wyoming	0.00%	5.33%
Mississippi	5.00%	5.71%			
Missouri	6.00%	5.79%			
Montana	11.00%	6.25%			

*Source: Federation of Tax Administrators
** State income tax is limited to dividends and interest only

Find the state that you live in and look at the break-even column. For example, if you live in the state of Arkansas, you will need to make a total return on your investment of 5.83% just to keep up with inflation and taxes. Keep in mind this chart is for illustrative purposes only. The numbers are based on a 4% inflation rate according to the Bureau of Labor Statistics' Consumer Price Index. It is derived from an averaged inflation rate for a 50-year period ending 12/2002. The rates also reflect a 25% federal tax rate. If you are in the top tax bracket, your break-even rate will be higher. If you want to calculate your exact break-even rate based on your current federal tax rate *and* you are an Algebra wiz, here is the formula:

$$\frac{\text{Inflation Rate}}{1-(\text{Maximum State Tax Rate} + \text{Federal Tax Rate})} = \text{Return}$$

(To be honest with you, my 14 yr old daughter Brittney had to do this for me.)

It might be good to check a state's tax rate if you are planning to move there. Montana has the highest state tax rate in the Union. Several states have 0. It's just a consideration.

Your retirement will invariably come up against three ice burgs.

1. Interest rate fluctuation
2. Taxes
3. Inflation

A. INTEREST RATE FLUCTUATION

With the market coming out of its third longest and second deepest bear market in history, interest rates have taken a beating reaching 40-year lows. For the first time in history the feds cut interest rates eleven times in ONE year. What goes down must come up when it comes to cyclical markets. Look for the feds to raise rates periodically over the next two years.

"Why do the feds raise and lower interest rates anyway?" That is a really good question. You are getting good. I'll try to make this as plain and painless as possible. It really is quite simple though.

- *Feds lower rates*

Over the past two years the feds have consistently lowered the interest rate on the US Central Bank's short-term rates. Greenspan's rational for doing this stems from his attempt to jump-start the economy. Why? In this case it is due to the recent recession. A recession is, in simple terms, when an economy that had previously been growing, slows down. The level of production declines, unemployment rises and consumer spending dries up. If these negative economic conditions continue for more than six months it is considered a recession. If the downturn continues for a long period of time, the condition could be classified as a depression.

What the feds try to do is make money easy to get. When rates are low, loans are up. When loans are up, disposable (spendable) money is more available. When disposable money is abundant, people start buying more. When people start to buy more, companies start expanding. When companies start expanding, unemployment begins to decline. Add all this up and it equals a growing economy.

For example, when short-term fed rates are low, the cost of borrowing money becomes cheaper, which means that people who owe a lot of money (for example in a mortgage) are able to refinance at a better rate, pull out equity, and have more cash in their pockets. Those who don't are more likely to take out new loans. Businesses are able to expand with cheap loans, too, and create more jobs. Cutting interest rates also gives a boost to share prices since the money (interest) that an investor can make in a fixed rate bank account becomes much, much less than in the stock market, thus making the stock market more attractive for investors.

- *Feds raise rates*

Mr. U. R. Loco owns a computer store. During the recession, he had 100 computers on his shelves and only ten customers, thus he had to lower his prices to draw more business. (In rare cases this can lead to deflation).

Now that rates are low and more money is available to consumers, Mr. Loco has 90 computers on the shelves and 110 customers who want to buy them. He is now in the driver's seat so he decides to raise his prices since demand is outpacing supply. Uh oh. Do you realize what just happened? I-N-F-L-A-T-I-O-N. That's right. His prices went up. What do we do now? We call Greenspan-Man! He swoops in and starts to raise interest rates, which is like turning a giant faucet down. The "easy" money is less plentiful which means, *ideally,* there will be about 90 customers for 90 computers thus keeping inflation in check.

You are now an expert on inflation and interest rate fluctuation. Wasn't that easy?

B. TAXES

Nothing in life is certain except death and taxes, and death doesn't get worse every time congress meets. Over 110 years ago at the 1893 Chicago World's Fair, the American Press Association asked 74 social commentators to look a century into the future and give their predictions of what life would be like. Would you like to hear some of those predictions? "Prisons and poorhouses will decline and divorce will not be considered necessary." "By the end of the 20th century, taxation will be reduced to a minimum, the entire world will be open to trade, and there will be no need for a standing army." Here's my favorite: "In 1993 the government will have grown more simple, as true greatness tends always toward simplicity."

Since these social commentators were a "little" off in

their predictions, taxes are a real threat to a retirement package. As an investment consultant in the business of selling securities, I am very limited in what I can promise. But one thing I can guarantee: your money will grow faster in a *tax-deferred* environment than it will in a taxable one.

C. INFLATION

We know all about the subject of inflation from chapter three now don't we? If so, why am I bringing it up again in this chapter? Two reasons: One, because the biggest obstacle to longevity in retirement is inflation, and I want to make sure you know your enemy well. Since it is not visible to the naked eye it can quietly erode the spending power of your money without you noticing. To reiterate how potent inflation is, I've included a simple illustration that further defines its severe effect on your long-term capital.

(Inflation rate of 4% annually)

Years to Retirement	Inflation Factor	Amount Required to Equal the Worth of $1 Saved Today
5	1.216	$1.22
10	1.480	$1.48
15	1.800	$1.81
20	2.191	$2.19
30	3.24	$3.24

This chart is a grim reminder of the potentially devastating effects inflation can have on future income.

The second reason to revisit this subject is to take your understanding to the next level. Most sea captains would agree that the biggest danger at sea, when fighting a powerful storm, is running out of fuel. A ship without power in a storm is at the mercy of the tempest. The biggest danger in retirement is running out of money before you run out of retirement. Who dies first, you, or your money?

The following chart is designed to show you just how

long your retirement dollars will last. The duration is based on the amount you take out verses the amount that goes in.

Withdrawal Rate	Expected Rate of Return											
	4%	5%	6%	7%	8%	9%	10%	11%	12%	13%	14%	15%
6%	27.6	35.9	*	*	*	*	*	*	*	*	*	*
7%	21.2	25.2	32.6	*	*	*	*	*	*	*	*	*
8%	17.4	19.7	23.2	29.8	*	*	*	*	*	*	*	*
9%	14.7	16.3	18.4	21.6	27.6	*	*	*	*	*	*	*
10%	12.8	13.9	15.3	17.2	20.2	25.7	*	*	*	*	*	*
11%	11.3	12.2	13.2	14.5	16.3	19.1	24.1	*	*	*	*	*
12%	10.2	10.8	11.6	12.6	13.8	15.5	18	22.7	*	*	*	*
13%	9.2	9.7	10.4	11.1	12	13.2	14.7	17.2	21.5	*	*	*
14%	8.5	8.9	9.4	10	10.7	11.5	12.6	14.1	16.3	20.4	*	*
15%	7.8	8.2	8.6	9.1	9.6	10.2	11.1	12.1	13.5	15.6	19.58	*

* = You will never run out of money with this combination of Earnings and Withdrawal amounts.

This chart shows the correlation between income and outgo. If you are withdrawing 7% of your money and, at the same time, are making 7% interest, you will never run out of money. However, we are vividly reminded that inflation will not allow us to merely take out what goes in without consequences. Drawing the same level of income, year after year, without adjusting for inflation will force you to reduce your standard of living. Be *sure* to keep this in mind.

Now, let's put this chart to some practical use. Based on the numbers you calculated in chapter three do the following. Take the grand total of your liabilities on page 90 and put it on line one.

_____

Line One
(Make sure you use the *annual* figure here)

Skip forward to chapter four and calculate your liquid assets (A + B + C) and put the amount on line two.

Line Two
_____

Get a calculator and divide the larger number on line two into the smaller number on line one. When you get the answer, move the decimal two spaces to the right. This is the percentage you will need to cover your current expenses. Now take that same percentage and find it on the chart above in the left column. In order to never run out of money, you will need to equal your outgoing percentage with the same incoming percentage. Let me reiterate again and again; although this percentage rate is the minimum you will need to always have a paycheck, this will *not* help you keep up with inflation and taxes. I can't stress this enough. (Can you tell?)

FIGURE EXAMPLE BELOW

You have expenses equaling $3,000 per month. Your assets, which are defined as any *income producing* investments you currently own, equal $500,000. Divide 3,000 by 500,000 = .006 now multiply .006 by 12 (the number of months you will need 3,000 in a year). .006 X 12 = .072 Move the decimal point to the right two spaces. .072 = 7.2%. You will need to draw 7.2% from your income producing investment funds to meet your monthly expenses. If your money is making 6%, then according to the chart above, your money will last approximately 32 years before it goes to 0. If your money makes 7.2% or better, not only will you never run out of money, (if the withdrawal rate remains 6% or less) but you will be able to raise your income each year.

II. YOUR LEVEL OF RISK TOLERANCE

Before you make an investment decision, you need to

consider how you *feel* about the prospect of your investment value going down. Of course no one feels good about losing money, but some can tolerate volatility better than others. It may be that to sleep better at night, you are willing to live on less income, which is perfectly fine. Keep in mind, however that *there is no such thing as a risk-free investment.* As I have illustrated in previous chapters, even CDs carry risk.

One of my clients told me she actually buried a bank bag full of money in her back yard. A few days later, she saw her dog running up to her with something in his mouth. It was, you guessed it, her bag of money! True story.

This just proves that even if you bury your money in the back yard, it's not entirely safe. Her dog could have eaten, lost, or reburied the bag somewhere else. It's in an account with me now.

Based on the investment return over the last 50 years, it is reasonable to expect the following *long-term* market performance above inflation:

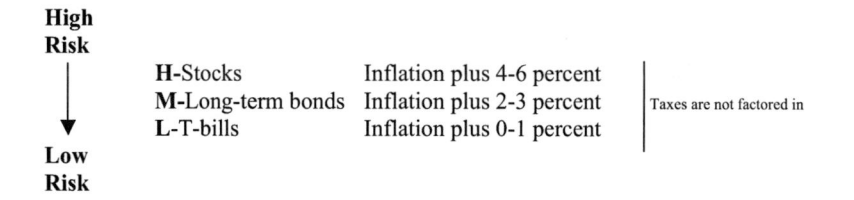

High Risk
↓
↓
Low Risk

H-Stocks	Inflation plus 4-6 percent
M-Long-term bonds	Inflation plus 2-3 percent
L-T-bills	Inflation plus 0-1 percent

Taxes are not factored in

Investment Approach

Now that you are armed with the right information, it is time to carefully consider the following questions to determine your **risk tolerance.**

Before we begin this exercise let me address one issue that will greatly influence your score. In a word, fear. The word "fear" comes from the Old English word, Faer, which means sudden danger. It refers to fright where fright is justified. It refers to danger that is concrete, real, and knowable. In such cases fear is appropriate, and sometimes useful, if one is to escape harm.

A Funny Thing Happened on My Way to Work . . . I Retired

This emotion comes as a result of *outside* influences. This type of fear is the least of our problems here, however.

We are more apt to be haunted by anxiety, worry, and dread. Anxiety comes from the Latin word, anxious, meaning a tight feeling in the chest. It is anxiety that stays with us even when there is no real, concrete, knowable stimulus. Anxiety comes as a result of being uncertain. It feeds on the "what ifs" of life. Anxiety comes not from without but from *within*.

What you will need to do, (and this will be difficult), is determine which emotion affects your risk tolerance. Is it fear or anxiety? Is it well-founded caution or is it worry because of the unknown? It is easy to listen to the doomsayers who predict nothing but bad news, but keep in mind; constant bombardment of negative advice can lead to unintended negative consequences.

Here is a story that has a lot to do with the current market anxiety. This story has been around for years and years. I've updated it a bit so that it fits right in with the point I am trying to make.

Here goes: A man lived by the side of the road . . . and sold hot dogs. He was hard of hearing, so he had no radio. He had trouble with his eyes, so he had no newspaper or TV and certainly no Internet access.

But he sold good hot dogs. He put up a sign on the highway, telling how good they were. He stood by the side of the road and cried, "Buy a hot dog, mister!" And people bought. He increased his meat and bun order, and he bought a bigger stove to take care of his trade. Then his son came home from college.

His son said, "Father, haven't you been watching TV or reading the newspapers? There's a big correction in the market. Corporations are guilty of horrible crimes. Surely there will be more terrorist attacks." Whereupon the father thought, "Well, my son has gone to college. He watches television and reads the newspapers, so he ought to know."

So, the father cut down on the bun order, took down his advertising signs, and no longer bothered to stand on the highway to sell hot dogs. His hot dog sales fell almost overnight. "You were right, son," the father said to the boy. "This problem in the market is certainly hurting. I'm glad we cut back."

Why did this happen to our hot dog dealer? The answer is obvious, he let the negative influence of his son raise his level of anxiety to the point it cost him his business. He should have told his son, "Good hot dogs always sell. Go get a job."

Don't make the mistake of basing your investment decisions on the negative news that is constantly spewed at you from the TV and newspaper industry. If you listen to and follow negative advise, *without getting all the facts,* you will run the risk of loosing your hotdog stand. I'm reminded of an episode on the sitcom "Gilligan's Island" where Gilligan makes a pair of wings out of some feathers. He climbs up on a hut and starts flapping. He finds himself hovering off the ground. He's flying! Suddenly the skipper looks up, sees what's happening and says, "Gilligan, you can't fly!" Gilligan responds, "I can't?" "No!" exclaims the skipper. Of course you know what happens next; Gilligan comes crashing to the sandy ground. As everyone runs over to see if he's ok, he looks at the skipper and says, "Why did you have to tell me I couldn't fly? Why?" Don't let people tell you that you can't fly! Buy quality investments and stay the course.

On the next few pages you will find a "risk tolerance" self test. Take your time on each question and read it thoroughly before going on to the next one. Select only one answer for each category. There are five categories, which means you will select a total of five answers.

1. INVESTMENT OBJECTIVE

Which of the following statements best describes your overall approach to investing in a post-retirement portfolio? Select only one answer from this category.

Points
1. ❑ Having a relative level of *stability* in my overall investment portfolio
2. ❑ Having income-producing investments for most of my assets but to try to *slowly increase* my portfolio's value by investing a small portion of my assets in higher risk market-based investments for relative stability.
3. ❑ Having income-producing investments for most of my assets but to invest a *small to moderate* portion of my assets in higher risk market-based investments for growth potential.
4. ❑ Having income-producing investments for most of my assets but to invest a *moderate* portion of my assets in higher risk market-based investments for growth potential.
5. ❑ Having an approximate *balance* between income-producing investments and higher risk market-based investments for growth potential.
6. ❑ Attempting to increase my portfolio's value by investing a *moderately large* portion of my assets in market-based investments for growth potential, while investing the balance in income-producing investments.
7. ❑ Attempting to increase my portfolio's value by investing a *large* portion of my assets in market-based investments for growth potential, while investing the balance in income-producing investments

Points
8. ❑ Attempting to increase my portfolio's value by investing *virtually all* of my assets for growth potential, while having very few income-producing investments

2. VOLATILITY

The value of most investments fluctuates from year to year and even more so over the short-term. How would you feel if an investment you had committed to for ten years lost 20% of its value during the first year? Again, select only one answer.

Points
1. ❏ I would be extremely concerned and would sell
2. ❏ I would be moderately concerned and may consider selling my investment
3. ❏ I would be somewhat concerned, but I probably would not consider selling the investment.
4. ❏ I would not be overly concerned, given my long-term investment philosophy

3. VARIATION

Realize that any market-based investment may move up or down in value over time. With which of the hypothetical portfolios below would you feel most comfortable?

Points	Initial Investment	year 1	year 2	year 3	year 4	year 5	Average Annual Return
1. ❏	$10,000	10,300	10,600	10,900	11,200	11,500	3%
2. ❏	$10,000	10,400	10,800	11,200	11,700	12,000	4%
3. ❏	$10,000	9,500	10,500	11,500	12,300	12,500	5%
4. ❏	$10,000	9,400	9,200	12,300	12,600	13,500	7%
5. ❏	$10,000	8,800	7,900	7,100	12,000	15,000	10%

4. ECONOMY–US

In general, your feelings about the U.S. economy over the next ten years are:

Points
1. ❑ Pessimistic
2. ❑ Unsure
3. ❑ Optimistic

5. ECONOMY–GLOBAL

In general, your feelings about the world economy over the next ten years are:

Points
1. ❑ Pessimistic
2. ❑ Unsure
3. ❑ Optimistic

Now, add up your total score from all categories. See the chart below to rate your risk tolerance.

III. Risk category

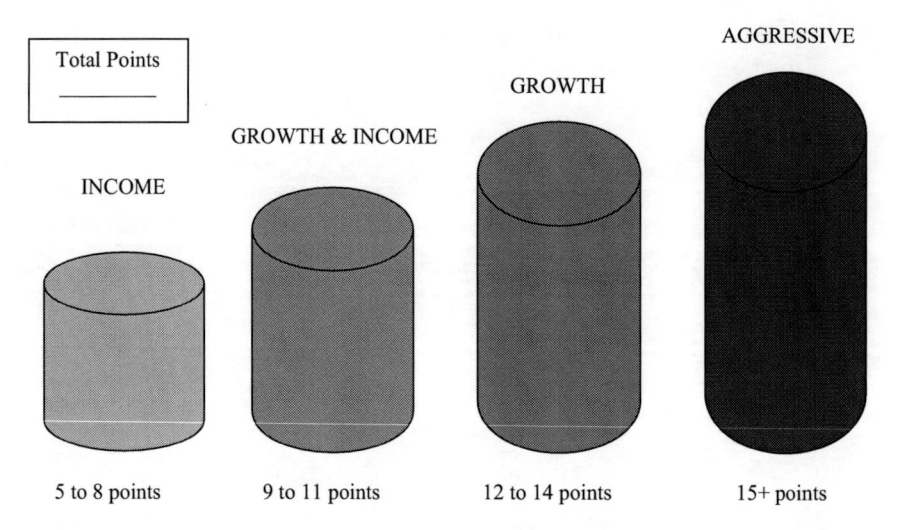

Total Points
_____

INCOME — 5 to 8 points
GROWTH & INCOME — 9 to 11 points
GROWTH — 12 to 14 points
AGGRESSIVE — 15+ points

Keep in mind that this self-test is broad in its approach. Its purpose is to give you a general idea about your risk tolerance. To fine-tune your score, ask your financial advisor for a more comprehensive test.

III. PORTFOLIO MIX

The following portfolio combinations are examples of different mixes for different risk tolerances, and for various investment goals. To create an appropriate portfolio blend for your investment needs, talk to a financial advisor. Although these suggestions are generally correct, I encourage you to seek a custom plan that fits you specifically. When it comes to investing, one size does *not* fit all.

INCOME:
Conservative: 20% Stocks
                  80% Bonds

Security is your greatest concern. You would not feel comfortable if your portfolio value fluctuated greatly.

GROWTH AND INCOME:
Balanced: 60% Stocks
               40% Bonds

Growth and security are both important to you and you want to pursue them in a somewhat equal measure.

GROWTH:
Expansion: 80% Stocks
               20% Bonds

Seeking growth of your money is your main concern, but you prefer to limit your potential risk.

AGGRESSIVE GROWTH:
High Risk: 100% Stocks
              0% Bonds

You seek to maximize growth of capital over the long

A Funny Thing Happened on My Way to Work . . . I Retired

run and you are comfortable with the potential risk and volatility that may occur in the short run.

Ok. Let's say, after you take this test, you discover that you simply have no tolerance for investment risk. You cannot see yourself putting money into any of the four portfolio combinations I've just outlined. Are you out of options? No! There is still hope. No one is condemning you.

If you are one of the many investors who have absolutely no stomach for risk in the stock market, you are not alone. In fact, very few people have *total* invulnerability toward market risk. The psychologist Erickson contends that the most basic need of an infant is the development of a sense of trust. That is the most basic need of every adult as well. Trust is something learned over time. I have many clients who can't seem to get to the point where they "trust" the fact that the market will return more than it takes. So, before you throw up your hands and retreat back into the "safe" cave of CDs, let me offer one more idea that can give you some growth and still give you the assurance you require. I believe even the most timid investor can do this if he understands it. It is a technique known as "interest averaging."

That being said, there are investors who seem to thrive on taking chances with their investments. They are like the tightrope walkers without a net:

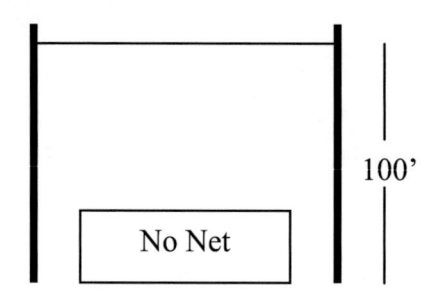

100'

No Net

These types of mavericks don't mind taking risks in the market. Not many investors are like this and for a very good reason. Most day traders would fall into this category. Don't feel bad if you're not one of them. Neither am I.

Next, there are investors who are willing to take *some* risks but still need some guarantees before putting any significant money into the market.

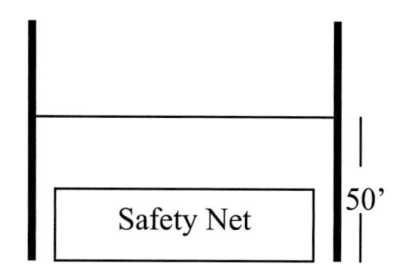

```
|                              |
|   ┌──────────────┐           |
|   │  Safety Net  │   50'     |
|   └──────────────┘           |
|                              |
```

Finally, there are those (you may be one) who have no desire or tolerance for market risk at any level. Up to this point their only option has been to "hide" their money in CDs or T-bills. Take heart. I have an investment strategy that may satisfy anyone's need for safety *and* stability and offer growth, all at the same time. Sound Impossible? Let's see.

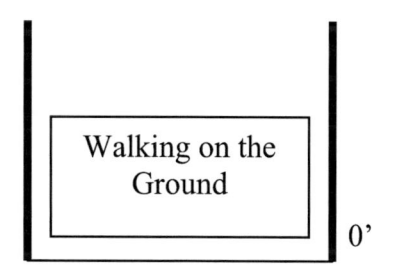

```
|                              |
|   ┌──────────────┐           |
|   │ Walking on the│          |
|   │    Ground    │           |
|   └──────────────┘   0'      |
```

As I mentioned earlier, this method is called *Interest Averaging*. Interest averaging is a strategy that can be used to offset investment risk. I recommend this method of investing to my risk-shy clients. It works like this: The investor puts a select amount of money into a fixed account such as a bond, fixed annuity or a fixed account inside a variable annuity. This will yield a fixed return annually with little or no risk to your principal. The interest rate will be constant for most fixed investments allowing for a consistent rate of appreciation. Most insurance companies guarantee the fixed accounts in their variable annuities and offer a minimum interest rate (some are currently at 3%) that can go up every twelve months in the event interest rates rise. While keeping the principal safe, you let the *interest* from the fixed account dollar-cost-average into the variable side of the annuity, i.e. the market. You have now eliminated the risk on your principal and you have systematically invested the gains into the market where some of your money *needs* to be. I've included a simple illustration of how a variable annuity utilizing interest-averaging works. (Don't confuse this illustration with a fixed annuity. A fixed annuity is much like a tax-deferred CD in that it can't do anything but draw interest. This variable annuity has a fixed account in it but it can do much more).

VARIABLE ANNUITY

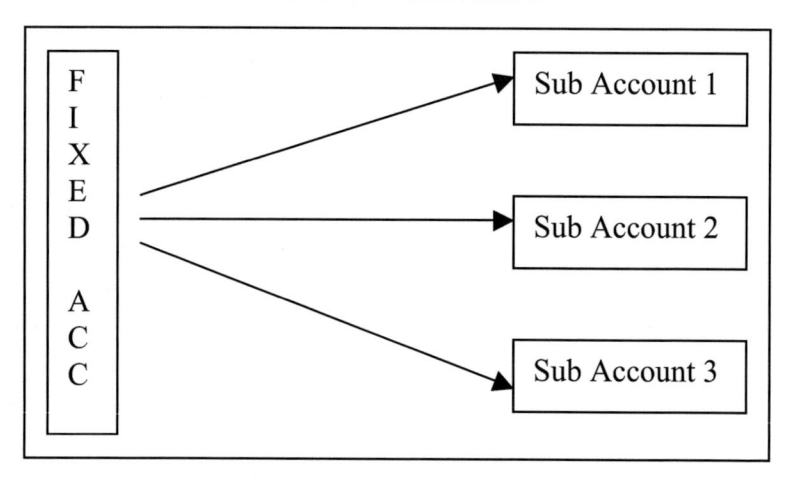

```
┌─────────────────────────────────────────────┐
│  ┌───┐                    ┌──────────────┐  │
│  │ F │─────────────────▶  │ Sub Account 1│  │
│  │ I │                    └──────────────┘  │
│  │ X │                                      │
│  │ E │                    ┌──────────────┐  │
│  │ D │─────────────────▶  │ Sub Account 2│  │
│  │   │                    └──────────────┘  │
│  │ A │                                      │
│  │ C │                    ┌──────────────┐  │
│  │ C │─────────────────▶  │ Sub Account 3│  │
│  └───┘                    └──────────────┘  │
└─────────────────────────────────────────────┘
```

The initial investment is kept in the fixed account, which is protected from market volatility and is guaranteed by the insurance company not to loose value. . The interest that is earned in the fixed account is moved from the fixed account into a sub account that *is* subject to market volatility but is also exposed to greater growth potential.

The example below is the historical performance of an account that actually utilized this method. In other words, these figures really happened.

End of Year	Initial Investment	Interest transferred Over 12 months	Cumulative Account Value	Contract Value	Interest Rate of Return
12/88	$100,000	$2,651	$2,702	$102,702	-----
12/89	$100,000	$7,892	$11,801	$111,801	8.86%
12/90	$100,000	$7,672	$18,880	$118,880	6.33%
12/91	$100,000	$7,016	$30,688	$130,688	9.93%
12/92	$100,000	$5,516	$39,302	$139,302	6.59%
12/93	$100,000	$4,244	$48,931	$149,931	6.91%
12/94	$100,000	$4,244	$51,603	$151,603	1.79%
12/95	$100,000	$4,756	$73,854	$173,854	14.68%
12/96	$100,000	$4,468	$95,484	$195,484	12.44%
12/97	$100,000	$4,372	$128,709	$228,709	17.00%
12/98	$100,000	$4,180	$174,466	$274,466	20.01%
12/99	$100,000	$3,924	$210,688	$310,688	13.20%
12/00	$100,000	$3,972	$197,196	$297,196	-4.34%
12/01	$100,000	$4,020	$174,833	$274,833	-7.52%
	Fixed Accumulation Feature Value	Total Interest Transferred	Total Stock Account Value	Total Contract Value	Average Interest Rate of Return
	$100,000	$69,908	$174,674	$274,674	7.72%

This person realized an annual return of 7.72% in spite of the fact that he accepted a lower interest payout as a result of lowered risk. Remember our example earlier in this chapter under the inflation section? We discovered that we needed a 7.2% return to keep our portfolio from running out of money. With interest averaging we have "mission accomplished." Not only are we able to draw a better return on our money with this strategy, but we also are able to lessen the impact of inflation. Imagine, two birds with one stone and we actually lowered our level of risk! (This guy is good)!

Let me reiterate that this is only for those who cannot endure the unpredictability of the market. Those who can stomach some movement (no pun intended) would have done much better by putting a generous portion of the $100,000 to work in the market in 1988. (Don't break out in a cold sweat; it's just something to think about).

Let's do a benefit recap of interest averaging:

1. **Preservation of Initial Investment**
   All of the assets in the fixed accumulation feature are guaranteed by the insurance company not to go down.

2. **Reduced Volatility**
   Only the interest that has been averaged into the investment options is subject to market volatility, not the initial investment, it remains fixed. Just remember one thing when it comes to market swings, if the market lost more than it made, like some people believe, it would be at zero today! Therefore, a prudent person must conclude that the market gains more than it looses . . . again, just something to think about.

3. **Systematic Investing**
   Steady, consistent investing offers the potential to purchase securities during the market's ups and downs, making the volatility work for you. How? By purchasing more shares when prices are low and fewer shares when prices are high resulting in ownership of securities at a lower average unity price, also known as dollar-cost-averaging.

IV. FIVE WAYS TO EASE TAXES IN RETIREMENT

Thus far we've explored some of the pitfalls associated with investing in the stock market. We discussed, at length, the roll inflation plays in our investment decisions. Now I want to shift gears and offer some tips that can help soften the impact of taxes on your portfolio. I have had some good results with these strategies.

1. ACCESS THE EQUITY IN THE HOME

Having equity in your home is Like Wall Papering your home with $100 bills. It is *Lazy* Money!

If you are young and currently *saving* for retirement, I suggest you keep your equity intact for now. However, if you are at the age of retirement and you have a large portion of your home equity loan paid off, think about this: Equity in the home does not grow by one cent in value. Your house will appreciate or depreciate whether there is equity in the home or not.

Let's look at an example. A retiree has a home that appraises for $250,000. They owe $50,000 on the note. They have $200,000 in equity sitting in a "growth-free" environment. Let's say this retiree takes my advice and refinances with an interest only loan. This is a loan that only requires you to pay interest back with no principal, causing your payments to be much lower. Now you have access to $200,000 TAX-FREE dollars to use toward retirement.

I know what some of you are thinking. I talk to many retirees who rank paying off their home as one of the top priorities on their to-do list. My question is WHY? If you pay off your home you will eliminate a very important tax right off. Since I'm sure you don't want to give your children a house with no equity in it, secure mortgage or term insurance to pay off the balance when you die. An excellent book to read regarding accessing your equity is *Missed Fortune* by Douglas R. Andrew. It will explain in great detail what I am talking about here.

2. LOWER YOUR TAXABLE INCOME

Wouldn't it be great if it were that simple? It just might be. Let me explain.

Roll qualified money into a fixed annuity. Keeping your

qualified money in a tax-deferred environment can lower your tax bill each year. Why a fixed annuity? Fixed annuities:

- Are free from stock market risk
- Generate tax-deferred earnings
- Lower Social Security tax liability
  (Gains in a fixed annuity do NOT add to your provisional income)
- Allow this portion of your estate to avoid probate
- ***Can be borrowed against for tax-free income or to start a new business (for non-qualified money only)***

EXAMPLE:

You retire with a $300,000 401k.

- Option one: You can take lump sum distribution
   *Pay $60,000 in tax (Not advisable)
- Option two: Roll into IRA and take distributions
   * Remember, our withdrawal rate must not out pace our interest rate

As I have stressed throughout this book, these investment examples are used for illustrative purposes only. Consult your financial advisor before purchasing any investment security.

3. LOWER YOUR INCOME TAX

Again, this sounds easier said than done, but not necessarily. Go back to the **"Let's Start Building the Ship"** chapter and review the form you filled out to calculate your retirement income. Note the different *sources* that produce your income. Here is an important tip: Any source that pays income through dividends and long-term capital gains can reduce your year-end tax bill.

Example: A single retiree has an annual income of

$35,000 coming from bonds, CDs and an IRA. He is in the 28% tax bracket.

>Example I: 28%
>Taxable Income: $35,000
>Tax (Single): $5,494
>Total Tax = $5,494

Let's take the same individual with the same income. This time, however, he adjusts his income sources so that $10,000 of his income comes from dividends and long term capital gains.

>Example II: 28%
>Income: $35,000
>Taxable Income: $25,000 = $3,396
>*Capital Gains:* $10,000 = *$1,500*
>**$4,896**

Now, instead of a $5,494 tax bill, the retiree has a $4896 tax bill. His total bill has been reduced by $598. How? The maximum long-term capital gains can be taxed is 15%. Our retiree is in the 28% tax bracket so moving a portion of his income to a dividend paying security caused a portion of his income to be taxed at a lower rate. Talk to your tax advisor before making any changes in your portfolio.

4. RAISE YOUR INCOME

One good way to maintain steady and dependable investment income is to purchase a series of bonds, CDs, or annuities with staggered maturities. We call this an *Income Ladder*. For example you could purchase a bond that matures after one year, another one that matures after two years, another one that matures after three years and so on. Since it is true that a five-year bond generally pays higher interest than a one-year bond, it would be to your benefit to purchase fixed investments with longer maturities. But, keep this in mind; if interest rates move up, we could be locked in to a low interest rate if we go out too far on the maturity. The solution? Laddering.

First, we buy the following bonds. (Fixed annuities and CDs will work here too).

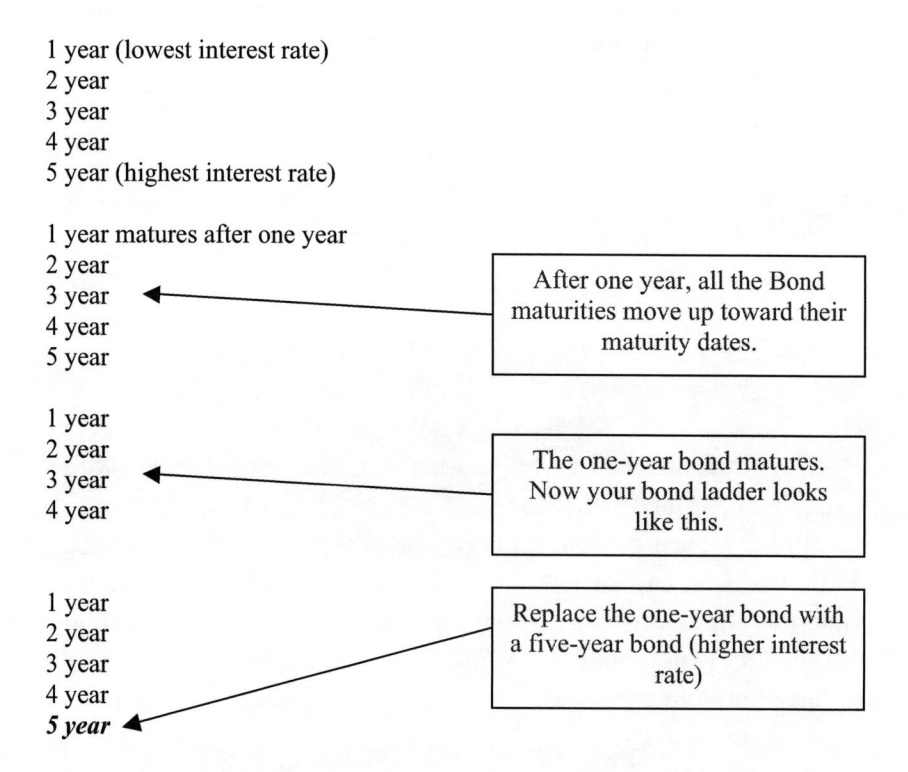

1 year (lowest interest rate)
2 year
3 year
4 year
5 year (highest interest rate)

1 year matures after one year
2 year
3 year ← After one year, all the Bond maturities move up toward their maturity dates.
4 year
5 year

1 year
2 year
3 year ← The one-year bond matures. Now your bond ladder looks like this.
4 year

1 year
2 year
3 year
4 year
5 year ← Replace the one-year bond with a five-year bond (higher interest rate)

Keep repeating this system until all of your bonds have five-year maturities. You will still have one bond that will mature every year, which will help you avoid locking up all your money in a low-interest bearing investment for an extended period of time.

5. KNOW WHEN TO SELL

"Buy low and sell high!" You've heard this before and you know it is a lot harder to do than it sounds. After all, when is a good time to buy stocks? When everyone is running away from the market in stark terror. Conversely, when is the best time to sell? When every one is euphoric thinking the bubble will never burst. The only way to take emotion out of the buying and selling process is to use a qualified financial advisor who can help temper your decision with some common sense. Of course the ultimate decision will be yours but a second opinion at the height of emotion can save a thousand regrets.

CONCLUSION:

These portfolio mix suggestions are meant to be just that, suggestions. There is always room for adjustments based on your particular needs. Be sure to consult your Captain (Advisor) before purchasing any securities. If you scored low on risk tolerance but feel you need a better return than what that category yields, give yourself time to learn and adjust. You don't have to be "stuck" on one level forever.

Some people live on the level of constant fear that somewhere "out there" lurks something tragic that is going to happen to them or someone they love. One night, a man was abruptly awakened by his wife. She was sure she heard a burglar downstairs. He slowly got up, went grumpily downstairs, and found himself staring into a gun. The burglar ordered him to hand over all the household valuables, and then started to leave. The husband stopped him. "Before you go," he said, "I'd like you to come upstairs and meet my wife. She's been expecting you every night for over 30 years."

If the inevitable happens, and you learn not to worry about it, at least you will have gotten a good night's sleep for 30 years.

In the event I am preaching to the choir, let me address the other side of extreme risk tolerance. On Thursday, August 13, 1992, David Kaplan, a producer for ABC News was shot while on assignment in Bosnia. There are a couple of alarming facts about his death: First of all, those correspondents who had arrived to cover the news in Bosnia were to be transported in an *armored vehicle;* David Kaplan refused, and instead chose to ride in an unprotected jeep. In the second place, all journalists were to wear a *bulletproof vest* for protection; David Kaplan did not have his on at the time. Reports showed there had been no sniper fire that morning, and the **chances** were that everything would be fine. And so David Kaplan let down his guard, forgetting for a moment that the area had been declared a war zone, and it cost him his life.

You may have such an immunity to fear that you take dangerous risks. Kaplan could have arrived at his destination just the same if he had taken some precautions. They might have slowed him down, but he might still be alive today.

Today's world market is a war zone. We have to prepare for dangers our grandparents never dreamed of. We are the first generation to have to worry about outliving our resources. We need to prepare for the unimaginable. As Winston Churchill said: "Let our advance worrying become advance thinking and planning."

The best safety precautions I can offer to any investor, no matter what level of risk tolerance they're on, are summed up in three rules: diversify, diversify, and diversify.

"Let's just be thankful we're not getting all the government that we're paying for."

- Will Rogers

CHAPTER FIVE

WHAT IS YOUR "NET" WORTH?

The wolves were decimating the farmers' sheep so the authorities raised the bounty on them. Two hunters decided they could use the extra money. They headed out to the wide-open spaces to shoot some wolves and make themselves rich! They had just fallen asleep out under the stars when a noise woke one of them. In the reflection of the campfire he saw the eyes of twenty-five wolves with teeth gleaming. He shook his friend and whispered hoarsely; "Wake up! Wake up! We're rich!"

Since people obviously have different views of wealth, we need to determine what your net worth is and make a correct analysis to determine its true value.

What is net-worth worth? Someone once said, "It pays not to leave a dragon out of your plans especially if you happen to live near one." You may or may not come upon a "dragon" in your retirement years but it pays to have a contingent plan just in case. Up to this point we have been building such a plan.

Some of you may be thinking, "This is too much like work!" but don't give up! This kind of *work* will pay dividends for the rest of your life. Besides, most of the work ahead is a one-time exercise, so keep digging for the gold.

Once there was a rusty old pickax stuck in the rocky wall of an unproductive mine, left there by a miner who had given up in disgust and walked away from it. Years later another miner idly swung his pick against the same wall and broke through into the fabulous Comstock Lode. Untold wealth had been waiting for the first miner if only he had persisted a little longer.

Keep swinging my friend!

A Funny Thing Happened on My Way to Work . . . I Retired

In this chapter we will discuss:

- Net worth
- Liquid Assets
- Securities
- Tax Deferred Assets
- Real Estate and Durables
- Liabilities

NET WORTH

What is "Net Worth?"

A net worth statement is a snapshot of your current financial situation, and will give you important clues about where you should concentrate your financial retirement planning efforts.

Your net worth is the difference between all the things of value that you own, and all the debts you owe. In financial terms, *your net worth is your assets minus your liabilities.* If you have more assets than liabilities, you have a *positive net worth*. This is a good thing. If you have more liabilities than assets, you have a *negative net worth*. This is not such a good thing, especially if you are heading into retirement, but its information you need to know either way.

In a PEANUTS cartoon, Lucy says: "Look at this tiny little bug. It's appalling how little he knows . . . he's not like us . . . he doesn't know anything about voting or disease or Earthquakes or love or Monday mornings!!"

Linus asks: "Who's better off?"

You may not feel better off once you discover your net worth but keep this objective in mind: Once you have established where you are, the journey to get where you want to be is half over. (Yours truly).

At one point in "Alice in Wonderland," Alice says to the Cheshire cat, "Would you please tell me, which way I ought to go from here?"

"That depends a good deal on where you want to get to," replies the cat.

"I don't care much where," Alice says.

"Then it doesn't matter which way you go," says the cat.

What should your goal be? You should set out to increase your net worth every year through a combination of new savings, investment profits and debt reduction. It can be useful to look at each category to determine your progress. Why track your progress? If you haven't already discovered, (and I know you have), the only guarantee in life that is consistent, other than death and taxes, is the fact that *nothing stays the same.* Whatever your net worth is when you begin retirement, you must plan to lower the liability side as time goes on. The reason for this is due to the cost of living, i.e. inflation and taxes. (Oh no, not again!)

There are basically two ways to increase your income as you travel through retirement, 1: Increase your positive cash flow, 2. Decrease your expenses. Having a clear, updated picture of your debt to equity ratio lets you calculate your progress toward debt-free status. Thus, you have decreased your expenses, which means you get to keep more. Add to this the growth of your money (if you are properly allocated) and you will enjoy a retirement that gets better and better financially.

You should update net worth figures at least once a year or every time a major financial change occurs.

(1): Let's begin with the current value of your entire portfolio by adding up all of your *assets*. (Things you own that have cash value). Note; don't make any discounts on the value as you complete this exercise. Example: If the value of an object is $100 and you paid $50 for it, omit the cost here and put $100 in the asset section. We will subtract the $50 in the liability section later.

A Funny Thing Happened on My Way to Work . . . I Retired

Liquid Assets	Current Value
Cash on Hand	$
Checking Balance	
Money Market Fund	
CDs	
U.S. Savings Bonds	
Savings Accounts	
Cash Value in Life Insurance Policies	
Other:	
Other:	
Other:	

Total_____ (A)

Steve Kiefer

Securities	Current Value
Stocks	$
Stock Funds	
Mutual Funds	
Bonds	
REITS	
Variable Annuities	
Fixed Annuities	
401(K)	
403(B)	
457	
Personal IRA(s)	
Pensions	
Profit Sharing	
Other:	
Other:	
Other:	

Total_____ (B)

Tax-Deferred Assets	Current Value
Traditional IRA	$
SEP/Simple	
401k/403b	
Profit Sharing	
Roth IRA	
Tax-Sheltered Annuity	
Equity in Company Pension Plan	
Other:	
Other:	
Other:	

Total_____ (C)

Real Estate and Durables	Current Value
House's Full Value	$
2nd or Vacation Home	
Rental Property	
Vehicles	
Personal Property, Jewelry, etc.	
Collectibles, Antiques	
Recreation Equipment	
Other:	
Other:	
Other:	

Total_____ (D)

Now add A, B, C, and D together:_____
Total Assets

(2): You are doing great! Now let's add up our total *liabilities*. In this section I am looking for your balances due. Note: Do not include any ongoing payments here. That came earlier. Example: If you have a boat and you *owe* $10,000 on it, put $10,000 in the following exercise. If your *payments* are $200 a month, *DON'T* put that here. :

A Funny Thing Happened on My Way to Work . . . I Retired

Liabilities (What you Owe)	Total Balance Due
Primary Home Mortgage	$
2nd or Vacation Home Mortgage	
Rental Property Mortgage	
Vehicles Loans Outstanding	
Credit Card Balances	
Cash Loans	
Business Loans	
Student Loans	
Bank/Personal Loans	
Taxes Owed	
Other:	
Other:	
Other:	

Total _____
Total Liabilities

We're almost there. Now subtract the total liabilities from the total assets. Put your answer here:_____.
CONGRATULATIONS!
You have just calculated your entire Net Worth. As I mentioned earlier, this figure is extremely important, and it changes frequently so keep your Net Worth calculations current.

CONCLUSION:

This is probably the most "un-fun" chapter in the book, but oh, so necessary. Let me say that having a negative net worth does not mean your retirement plans are dead, *if* you have a substantial, secure income source. Otherwise, you should seriously reconsider your exit date. Also, if you have a positive net worth, make sure it is significantly positive. I wish I could give you a ratio to go by here but there are too many variables out there for me to make an accurate assessment for all of my readers. The best way to determine the practically of *your* net worth, as it relates to *your* retirement, is to, (yes, you know), sit down with a professional financial planner. Once you know what your "net" is worth, you can begin to sail toward your destination armed with indispensable knowledge.

Samuel Dill said in his *Roman Society in the Last Century of the Western Empire:* "The Roman Empire did not fall because of the disruptive influence of Christianity, or because of sheer moral weakness, but because of an intellectual complacency that *froze* the life-blood." Don't stop growing and you won't stop sailing.

"By working faithfully eight hours a day, you may get to be a boss and work twelve hours a day."

-Robert Frost

CHAPTER SIX

NINE TORPEDOES THAT CAN SINK YOUR SHIP AND HOW TO AVOID THEM

It's been said that there are only two pains in life; the pain of discipline and the pain of regret, and that discipline weighs *ounces* while regret weighs *tons*. Discipline is difficult, if not down right hard, but it helps us avoid the overbearing reality that we have damaged our future.

In this chapter we will look at nine torpedoes (mistakes) that can cost us dearly in retirement. Let's get right to work.

FIRE TORPEDO ONE: Picking a generic retirement plan instead of one that is designed specifically for your needs.

Carl A. Boyle, a sales representative, was driving home when he saw a group of young children selling Kool-Aid on a corner in his neighborhood. They had posted the typical hand-scrawled sign over their stand: "Kool-Aid, 10 cents." Carl was intrigued. He pulled over to the curb. A young boy approached and asked if he would like strawberry or grape Kool-Aid. Carl placed his order and handed the boy a quarter. After much deliberation, the children determined he had some change coming and rifled through the cigar box until they finally came up with the correct amount. The boy returned with the change, and then stood by the side of the car. He asked if Carl was finished drinking. "Just about," said Carl. "Why?" "That's the only cup we have," answered the boy, "and we need it to stay in business."

Beware of "packaged" retirement plans that are pushed by firms that need to make a sell in order to stay in business.

FIRE TORPEDO TWO: Procrastinating.

Only moments after prying open a window and stepping into a dark bedroom a burglar came face to face with a vicious looking Doberman Pincher. The burglar froze in his tracks. Once his eyes adjusted to the dark he noticed a parrot on the back of the dog which squawked "You're gonna get caught!" The burglar hesitated, then ever so carefully lifted an item off a dresser and put it in his sack. The dog watched every move. The parrot said, "You're gonna get caught!" Without any sudden or jerky movement the burglar then cleaned off the valuable items from the top of the dresser. The dog glared. The parrot said, "You're gonna get caught!"

The burglar quietly left the room, walked down the hallway, entered another room. The dog followed his every movement in the hall and the next room. The parrot squawked, "You're gonna get caught!" From room to room the dog paced right behind the burglar while the parrot annoyingly shouted, "You're gonna get caught! You're gonna get caught!" At last the burglar finished stealing the jewelry and cash he found in the master bedroom closet. The Doberman scrutinized every move of every muscle. The parrot said, "You're gonna get caught!"

Exasperated, the burglar finally bent down and picked up a shoe. He threw it at the bird and screamed, "You dumb parrot! Can't you say anything else?" The parrot fluttered away to avoid the shoe, and then said, "Sic 'em."

Don't delay in starting the process of planning for retirement or you will get caught. Often people in their fifties decide they want to retire at sixty. But they find they made the decision a little too late to achieve their target retirement date. Ideally, planning for retirement should start when you get your first full-time job. Very few people, though, even think about retirement while still in their twenties. Reality: At *least* ten years is a realistic time frame to put your financial and personal life in order before your actual retirement date. Any shorter a time period and "You're gonna get caught!" (Generally, the more time you give yourself, the better).

FIRE TORPEDO THREE: Not understanding how much income you'll need in retirement.

The key to a secure retirement is making sure your money lasts at least as long as you do. Most financial advisors, including yours truly, calculate that a retiree will need between 70 and 75 percent of his present income to sustain his current lifestyle in retirement. But many factors can bump this figure much higher. Below are four quick questions to ask yourself as you go through this section.

A. THE FIRST QUESTION IS "HOW LONG CAN YOU EXPECT TO LIVE?"

While you're calculating how much annual income you'll need, you should also think about how many years your retirement will last. Americans are retiring earlier and living longer than ever before.

You could live a very long life. Usually, retirement income needs are based on a person's life expectancy. According to actuarial projections, a man who lives to age 65 can expect to live another 15 years. A woman can expect to live another 19 years. (See chart below)

Life Expectancy by Current Age

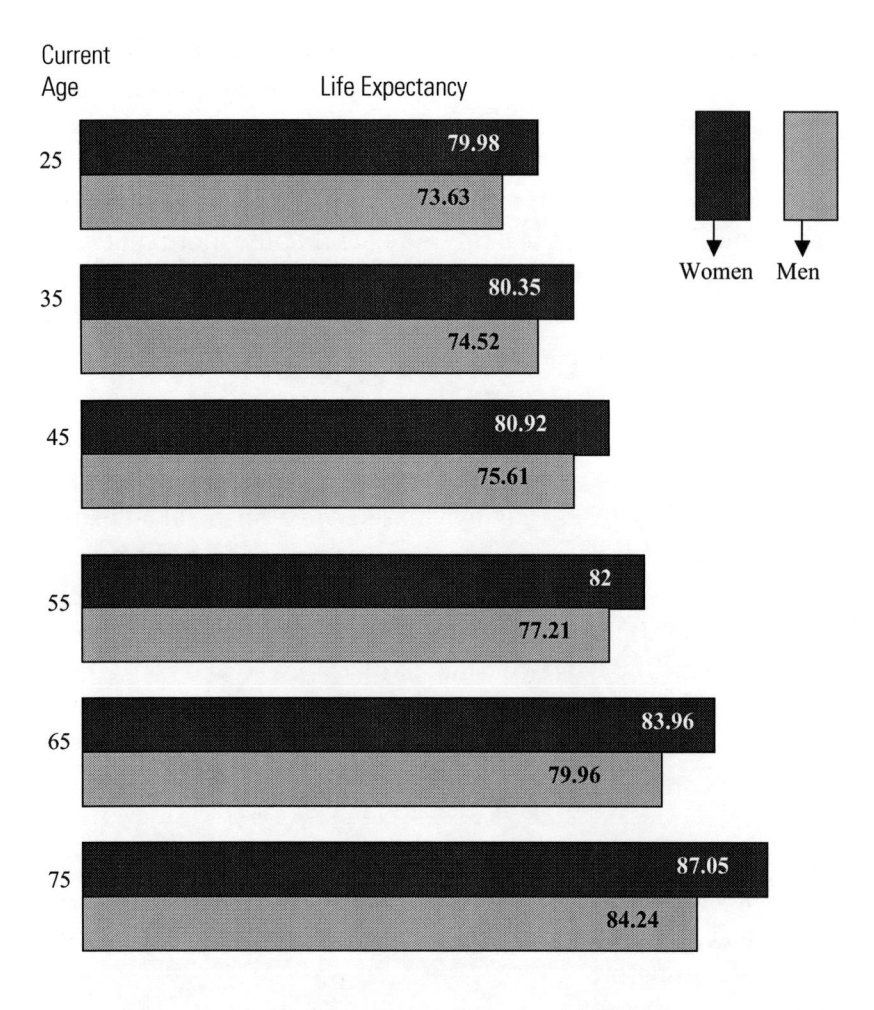

Current Age	Women	Men
25	79.98	73.63
35	80.35	74.52
45	80.92	75.61
55	82	77.21
65	83.96	79.96
75	87.05	84.24

But the number of persons reaching the age of 100 is growing impressively. You could be one of those who live beyond the century mark. You'd certainly want your income to see you through if this happened. (If you would like a more precise figure regarding your life expectancy, look at the Uniform Distribution Table in Chapter seven).

B. THE SECOND QUESTION IS "WHO WILL YOU NEED TO SUPPORT?"

Not only will you need an income, you may discover that

you need to provide financial assistance to others. Adult children . . . your siblings and/or parents may turn to you for help.

Jimmy came out of the bathroom and asked, "Whose is the pink toothbrush?" "Mine" His mother answered suspiciously, "Why? Did you drop it in the toilet?" "Yes" He answered, "But not today . . . yesterday." Yuck! No one likes unpleasant surprises. Make sure you have thought through this carefully. If you have aging parents and they do not have long-term care insurance, who is going to take care of them? Are you finished raising your children? In other words, have they completed college? Do you feel comfortable with your child's career choice? Of course, there is no way to predict all surprises, but taking some time to evaluate the "what if" scenario can mean the difference between a carefree retirement and a careless one.

C. THE THIRD QUESTION IS "HOW DO YOU WANT TO LIVE?"

Do you want to live better than you do now? The decision to travel a lot or buy a second home could boost your income needs in retirement over what they currently are.

Sometime back, in Sydney, Australia, a prisoner succeeded in escaping jail. He hid in the underpinning of a delivery truck that had stopped briefly in the prison. A few moments later, when the truck stopped, the prisoner dropped down to the ground and rolled outward to freedom. Unfortunately, he discovered that he was now in the courtyard of *another* prison five miles from the first.

Don't make the same mistake. Don't go from the burden of work to the burden of debt. Why did you have to work all of those years in the first place? It was due to the fact that you had to make a living, i.e. pay the bills. Excessive spending just before or during retirement can put you in a pressured situation that can force you to delay retiring or can compel you to step back into the workforce. Set a budget you can live with and stick to it. While most retirees enjoy a significant drop in expenses when they retire, some, due to travel and vacation properties, actually see an increase in their expenses. Be careful here.

D. THE FORTH QUESTION IS "WHERE DO YOU WANT TO LIVE?"

Two felons on death row were talking. One said, "Hey, it could be worse. We could be in a nursing home." (Mark Russell).

A woman had taken her elderly, fiercely independent mother to visit a retirement complex. She hoped to convince her of the advantages of living there instead of being alone in the old family home. "Mother, see how much fun they're having playing bridge," said the daughter cheerily. "While I'll bet when I'm their age, I'll love to live here too."

"Fine." The mother replied, "I'll be sure to visit you."

Obviously momma didn't want to live at the retirement complex, but, someday it may be a necessity for you and your family. When you can no longer live on your own but don't require nursing home care, you may need to consider an assisted-living housing arrangement that not only provides you with living quarters, but also with meals, housekeeping services, laundry, recreation and some on-site medical assistance.

Depending on where you live, assisted living costs can average $3,000 a month or more. Expect to see prices rise as baby boomers reach their 70s and 80s—starting in about 2016.

But, that is then and this is now. Where do you want to live after retirement? I just got back from the real estate office about 30 minutes ago. We just made an offer on a house that sits on the bank of Lake Conway. It is a three-bedroom two-bath structure that is about 2,200 square feet. The house needs some work so I am in hog heaven. (Remember my hobby is to build). If we get it, the property will serve as a weekend get-a-way for us now, but I plan to retire there in a few years. My plans may change, but for now that's where we want to live. Where do you want to live? If it fits your budget, go for it! The older you get the harder it will be to convince yourself to make such a move as this, so don't hesitate to make the change when you are free to do so.

FIRE TORPEDO FOUR:
Counting on Social Security alone.

You may have paid into the Social Security system for 30 years or more. While the system may be fiscally sound–for now–don't expect benefits to be substantial. At best, Social Security benefits only provide a safety net to retirement income. Currently, the most you can expect is about $1,500 a month. (Although this figure can rise the longer you wait to draw your Social Security check). If you want to retire early, before the normal retirement age fixed by law, your benefits will be permanently reduced.

Example: In the past, when the normal retirement age was 65, those retiring at 62 received a benefit reduced by 20%. Today, normal retirement age for someone born in 1938 is 65 years and two months. (See the chart on age increases in the chapter on Social Security).

If this person retires in 2000 at age 62, benefits are reduced by 20.83%. For those with a 67-year retirement age (starting in 2022), benefits will be reduced by 30% for those opting to take benefits starting at 62.

To get some idea of what to expect from Social Security when you plan to retire, you can use a quick benefits calculator on the Social Security Administration's Web site at: www.ssa.gov/retire/calculators.htm. I have also put this link on my website at www.stevekiefer.com for your convenience.

FIRE TORPEDO FIVE:
Underestimating medical costs.

Many believe that Medicare, a federal benefits program

covering many types of medical expenses starting at age 65, will cover everything. The truth is Medicare only covers *certain* medical expenses, *and* you must pay deductibles and co-payments on these expenses. In addition, Medicare does not cover out-of-pocket losses.

Alternative: You can deal with out of pocket and deductible expenses by carrying supplemental health insurance coverage known as *Medigap*. Costs vary according to the coverage you select. Keep in mind; this supplemental coverage does NOT cover extended nursing home or home health care expenses, which brings me to the next torpedo.

FIRE TORPEDO SIX: Failing to buy long-term-care insurance early.

Generally, Medicare doesn't cover the cost of long-term care that may be required by those with chronic diseases, such as Alzheimer's, dementia, or other old-age-related incapacities.

Can you afford it? The cost of long-term care is steep. Today's costs average about $50,000 annually nationwide and top out at $100,000 in some locations. Only a few can afford to pay for this kind of expense out of pocket. Keep in mind these figures are per year and not simply one-time payments. To illustrate: If you had $200,000 in savings, and you chose an average facility to stay in, your coverage would last approximately four years. After that, you would be broke and, unless you had additional assets, such as a home, you could be forced to turn to your family to take up the expenses.

Those with income and assets below modest, governmentally fixed levels, can qualify for Medicaid to cover nursing home costs, but don't expect the government to supply payments for a Beverly Hill's spa style nursing home. More importantly, anyone with assets to protect won't qualify for even the most basic governmental assistance in terms of long-term care needs;

therefore it is prudent to carry private long-term-care insurance. A word of caution here; don't try the gimmick of "giving" away your assets to your children before you go into a nursing home thinking the government will pick up the tab with Medicaid. It won't work. The government can go back three *or more* years to calculate your estate. Many people have tried this and many people have failed. You can't outsmart the government, at least not in this area. (Just kidding, Uncle Sam).

Historians have recently found the very first treaty the United States government ever signed with the Indians. The treaty states that the Indians can keep their lands "for as long as the river runs clear, as long as the buffalo roam, as long as the grass grows tall, and as long as the mountains stand proud—or ninety days—whichever comes first!"

But there is hope. Currently, you can gift cash and assets equal to $11,000 per year per child without any tax consequence for the giver or the recipient. This amount is up $1,000 from recent years.

Example: An only child receives $11,000 from her mom and $11,000 from her dad in the same year. What are the tax consequence to the giver and receiver? None. If you have two children, you and your spouse can give $44,000 a year away to them without incurring any tax. ($22,000 per child).

The younger you are when you take out the policy, the lower your annual premiums will be. You'll also avoid being denied coverage due to preexisting conditions. Example: Being diagnosed with diabetes can be a deal-killer with many long-term care insurance providers.

It's generally advisable to start this coverage in your late 40s to mid 50s. Good news: An increasing number of employers are offering this type of coverage. Ask your employer if they are one of them.

FIRE TORPEDO SEVEN:
Thinking you can retire early.

I don't want to be a cosmic killjoy here but I want you to think realistically. The stock market has recovered nicely over the past few months, which may have led you to believe that you now have enough money to retire on. Think again. These days, stock and stock option values change very fast. Review your finances carefully before you decide to quit your job.

A client told me of an individual who retired from a jet plane manufacturing job with $70,000 in his 401(k). Since the dot-com bubble was getting bigger at the time, he figured he could make this modest sum last a long time. Unfortunately, a very large popping sound was heard in March of 2000. The bubble burst and so did this individual's plans to stay retired. He was forced to go back to his old boss and beg for his job back.

A newspaper article in the spring of 1990 told an amusing story about a 42-year-old Ohio secretary who found herself running in a marathon. The problem was she thought she had entered a much shorter race. The two races were to begin minutes apart, and when the woman saw a crowd of runners all lined up to go, she simply hurried to join them.

She finished the marathon, but her tears and swollen knees will remind her to do more checking before she sets out the next time to run a race.

Retirement is not a sprint but a marathon. Make sure you have the resources to finish the race *before* you decide to start. Over the long haul, higher returns generally come from investments with higher degrees of risk. Still, hoping to earn unrealistic returns by putting all your funds in risky ventures is like driving too fast for road conditions. On the other hand, investing too conservatively out of fear of losing principal can actually create a loss due to inflation.

When the Hebrews were freed from their slavery in Egypt, they began a long journey to the "Promise Land." Some were young and strong and wanted to run to their new home. Others were old and weak and could barely walk. The solution was to set a pace that both young and old could live with. It worked.

The solution to maintaining a healthy retirement income is to run at a steady pace by diversifying your portfolio among several types of securities with various maturity dates. The best diversification strategy for you depends on how much time you have before you need the funds and how strong a stomach you have for riding the ups and downs of the market.

FIRE TORPEDO EIGHT:
Believing retirement will be nirvana.

Financial concerns are only one aspect of retirement. Many who retire early get bored and go back to work within a year or two, either on a voluntary basis or for pay. Decide how you're going to spend your time before you decide to retire.

In 1876 rumors were circulating that Sitting Bull had been killed. Warriors captured by the army denied this, however. Then army officers met with Sitting Bull and proclaimed him very much alive. A few months later, though, Sitting Bull and four other Indian chiefs came as a peace delegation to General Miles' camp and were slaughtered by Crow Indian scouts before the army realized what was happening. Finally Sitting Bull was dead, treacherously slain as he approached an army camp under a flag of truce.

But wait! Word came that Sitting Bull's camp no longer trusted the army and that Sitting Bull would no longer negotiate. Rumors persisted that Sitting Bull was alive, despite the army's possession of the dead chief's body.

Historians sorted the mess out a few years later. There were *two* different Sioux Indian chiefs named Sitting Bull. Sitting bull (from the Oglala Sioux) died in 1876. The more famous

Sitting Bull (from the Hunkpapa Sioux) did not die until several years later. Both men, though, were Sioux chiefs named Sitting Bull.

When I check in on my retired clients, I get very different responses to their retirement satisfaction. Although you will never know what it's like to be retired until you experience it for yourself, do your best to calculate the pros and cons in your planning, and above all, keep it realistic.

FIRE TORPEDO NINE:
Failing to seek expert guidance.

The late President Ronald Reagan enjoyed telling a story he said was true about a newspaper photographer out of Los Angeles who was called in by his editor and told of a fire that was raging out in Palos Verdes. That's a hilly area south of Los Angeles. His assignment was to rush down to a small airport, board a waiting plane, get some pictures of the fire, and get back in time for the afternoon edition.

Breathlessly, he raced to the airport and drove his car to the end of the runway. Sure enough, there was the plane waiting with the engines revved up, ready to go. He quickly climbed aboard. When they reached an altitude of five thousand feet, the reporter began getting his camera out of the bag. He told the fellow flying the plane to get him over the fire so he could take his pictures and get back to the paper. From the other side of the cockpit came a deafening silence. Then he heard these unsettling words: "Aren't you the instructor?"

Who is flying this thing? You may think retirement planning is a do-it-yourself process. But even if you're adept at handling your own investments, it is a good idea to review your plans with an expert. Find one who is proficient, i.e. one who has plenty of experience helping people make the transition from work to life (retirement).

This expert may bring up areas of concern you

have overlooked and can help you address them. Since retirement income planning isn't a one-time process, you need to review your plans regularly and make adjustments as situations and goals change. (Review the section on inflation if necessary).

A FEW CLOSING SALVOS

This is a word for those who still have many years before retirement.

When it comes to building a retirement nest egg, time is on your side. Even small amounts left to grow in a 401(k) or some other retirement-savings vehicle, will serve you more effectively than relatively larger amounts set aside in later years. Again, this is due to the fact that the funds in your retirement account, if left long enough, have the potential to grow through *compounding*. Let's say you save $100 a month and assume an 8% return. At the end of 26 years, you'll have an account balance of $99,600 and only $31,200 of this amount is your original contribution. The other $68,400 would be earnings!

Once you map out a course with a realistic retirement savings plan, the best way to achieve your goals is to stay the course. Losses incurred by trying to "time" the market can greatly diminish your returns. It's *time in the market, not timing the market,* say the experts. Missing out on just a few of the best days because of bad timing can be the difference between a positive return and a disaster.

The course to a sea of comfortable retirement lies ahead. And, with a little planning and discipline, the sail could be shorter than you think.

"All progress has resulted from people who took unpopular positions."

-Adlai E. Stevenson

CHAPTER SEVEN

AN UNEXPECTED ICEBERG

NOT WITHDRAWING ENOUGH

Things aren't always what they seem. When Richard Nixon ran for President in 1968, the Vietnam War was at its height. One of Nixon's TV commercials showed a photo of an American soldier in Vietnam with the word, "Love" written on his helmet.

The image bothered Harry Treleavan, one of Nixon's media men. "It reminds people of hippies," he said. "They don't think it's the sort of thing soldiers should be writing on their helmets."

About a week later, however, a letter arrived from the mother of the soldier. She described how thrilled she was to see the photo of her son in Nixon's TV commercial. She wondered if she could obtain a copy of the photo.

The letter was signed "Mrs. William Love."

(Gerald Tomlinson, *Speakers' Treasure of Political Stories, Anecdotes, and Humor,* (Englewood Cliffs, NJ: 1990).

Up until now I have been warning you about putting too much pressure on your retirement dollars by withdrawing too much from it. Well guess what? Some retirees are actually not taking enough out of their retirement nest egg. I am painfully aware of the dryness a worn out cliché' can bring, but this one really fits here. "Old habits are hard to break." It's true.

Example: I'd never heard of air conditioning while growing up on the farm in Indiana. When I went to church at Pleasant

A Funny Thing Happened on My Way to Work ... I Retired

Hills Methodist Church on Sunday mornings, my only air conditioner was a handheld fan donated by the local funeral home.

At night, my parents would put a box fan in the window down the hall from our bedrooms and it would hum all night sucking in the cool night air. (Are you getting sleepy?) To this day I can't sleep without a fan blowing. I even have one on now in my office as I am writing this book. I'm ashamed to say I have passed my addiction on to my wife and two children. We even take a fan with us when we go camping. Isn't that pathetic?

Spending retirement money can be a real challenge for people who spent most of their adult life saving up for it. I have clients whom I discovered were living just above poverty level while they had a $400,000 portfolio with me all along.

"So how can under-spending be bad for me?" At the risk of stating the obvious, retirement is supposed to be a time of rest and at least *some* self indulgence.

1. Realize that under-spending can lower the quality of life you have grown accustom to which can lead to other unpleasant consequences.

    The medical profession was slow to accept use of ether as an improved operating practice. Somehow the idea had been built up over the years that pain was a necessary and desirable part of the operating process.

    Another thing that undoubtedly slowed down the adoption of ether as an anesthetic was the fact that the first man to use it, Dr. Morton, wasn't a medical doctor. He was a dentist who had previously used ether to lessen the pain in extracting teeth. It took two more decades of needless pain before the medical profession, as a whole, got around to accepting the idea. Enduring hardships *unnecessarily* has no practical benefit to it whatsoever.

2. Realize that under spending can affect your loved ones in ways unintended. For many years Hetty Green was called

America's greatest miser. She can even be found in the Guinness Book of Records. When she died in 1916, she left an estate valued at $100 million, an especially vast fortune for that day, but she was so miserly that she ate cold oatmeal to save the expense of heating the water.

When her son received a severe leg injury, she took so long trying to find a free clinic that his leg had to be amputated because of advanced infection.

I certainly want you to be frugal in your finances when and where appropriate, but don't be miserly. I would rather you be like the man whose tombstone read, "He Took it With Him," than one that might read, "I Left It All for Someone Else to Spend." Certainly leave an inheritance for your children if it is possible, but not at the expense of a comfortable retirement. As a son, I would much rather see my parents spend their retirement money on themselves, than see them sacrificing through their golden years just so they can leave me something. I'm sure your children feel the exact same way.

3. Realize your current expenses will probably decrease when you retire due to the fact that employment has a financial price tag. With gas prices at all-time highs, just saving on travel expenses will be huge even if you don't drive that far to work. Other savings could be from not having to spend money on clothing, daycare, parking, meals, toll-fees, and other business expenses. A word of caution again; be careful not to replace one expense for another.

4. Realize that RMD is out there waiting for you. Many retirees don't know what RMD is. RMD is an acronym for *Required Minimum Distribution*. "OK, what exactly is that?" An RMD is a distribution amount that is required

A Funny Thing Happened on My Way to Work . . . I Retired

by the IRS for all participants in retirement accounts, (except the Roth), who are age 70½ and older.

Participants must receive at least a minimum amount for each year starting with the year in which he/she reaches age 70½. If the participant decides not to take an RMD in that first year, then the participant has until their Required Beginning Date (RBD), which is April 1st of the year following the year the participant turns 70½, to take their distribution. (Is your head spinning yet? Hang on. There's more). All RMD's thereafter must be taken by December 31st of each year. The distribution amounts are calculated based on the client's life expectancy, and on the prior year-end fair market value of their qualified holdings. Participants who do not satisfy the Required Minimum Distribution amount for any given year are required to pay a 50% excise tax on the amount not distributed. Required Distribution amounts are *not* eligible for rollover to another retirement account. ***Note: Contributions to the account must be discontinued once participants reach age 70½.***

Okay. Now that I have given you the 'Klingon' version of RMD, let me explain it in simple terms:

RMD is put in place by the IRS to make you take withdrawals from your traditional IRA. When you hit 70 and one half years of age, you will have to begin drawing down the amount.

Example: Mr. U. R. Wright has a traditional IRA that was valued at $132,941.36 on December 31, 2003. He is 74 years old. According to the life expectancy table, Mr. Wright is calculated to live for another 23.8 years. The equation is simple at this point.

$132,941.36 / 23.8 = $5,585.77

According to these figures, Mr. Wright will need to draw out cash and/or securities equaling $5,585.77 on or before

December 31, 2004. If he fails to do so, he will be fined 50% of the amount he was supposed to take out. Ouch!

Where did I get the figure 23.8? Look at the table below. Find your age in the left hand column. Move across to see your life expectancy. This is the new table being used by the IRS to determine RMD. Of course you don't have to be concerned about this until you reach age 70, but I want you to be aware of it now.

A Funny Thing Happened on My Way to Work . . . I Retired

Uniform Distribution Table

This table is the new life expectancy table to be used by all IRA owners to calculate lifetime distributions (unless your beneficiary is your spouse who is more than 10 years younger than you). In that case, you would not use this table, you would use the actual joint life expectancy of you and your spouse based on the regular joint life expectancy table. Keep in mind the Uniform Distribution Table is never used by IRA beneficiaries to compute required distributions on their inherited IRAs.

Age of IRA Owner or Plan Participant	Life Expectancy (in years)	Age of IRA Owner or Plan Participant	Life Expectancy (in years)	Age of IRA Owner or Plan Participant	Life Expectancy (in years)
30	66.6	59	37.8	88	12.7
31	65.3	60	36.8	89	12.0
32	64.3	61	35.8	90	11.4
33	63.3	62	34.9	91	10.8
34	62.3	63	33.9	92	10.2
35	61.4	64	33.0	93	9.6
36	60.4	65	32.0	94	9.1
37	59.4	66	31.1	95	8.6
38	58.4	67	30.2	96	8.1
39	57.4	68	29.2	97	7.6
40	56.4	69	28.3	98	7.1
41	55.4	70	27.4	99	6.7
42	54.4	71	26.5	100	6.3
43	53.4	72	25.6	101	5.9
44	52.4	73	24.7	102	5.5
45	51.5	74	23.8	103	5.2
46	50.5	75	22.9	104	4.9
47	49.5	76	22.0	105	4.5
48	48.5	77	21.2	106	4.2
49	47.5	78	20.3	107	3.9
50	46.5	79	19.5	108	3.7
51	45.5	80	18.7	109	3.4
52	44.6	81	17.9	110	3.1
53	43.6	82	17.1	111	2.9
54	42.6	83	16.3	112	2.6
55	41.6	84	15.5	113	2.4
56	40.7	85	14.8	114	2.1
57	39.7	86	14.1	115 & over	1.9
58	38.7	87	13.4		

Another major change in regards to RMD is the way it is now reported. There is a new box on form 5498 which tracks your IRA holdings and reports them to the IRS. Make sure you follow the guidelines in this book when you are approaching this age. If you are already over 70 and 1/2, go to my website, www.stevekiefer.com and click on calculators. You can go to the RMD calculator page and type in your date of birth and your IRA value as of December 31 of the previous year and it will calculate your RMD automatically for you.

The key to managing this issue is to siphon off money from the IRA gradually. This method can help you avoid an enormous tax burden later.

Attention:

This form is provided for informational purposes and should not be reproduced on personal computer printers by individual taxpayers for filing. The printed version of this form is designed as a "machine readable" form. As such, it must be printed using special paper, special inks, and within precise specifications.

Additional information about the printing of these specialized tax forms can be found in IRS Publications 1141, 1167, 1179, and other IRS resources.

The printed version of the form may be obtained by calling 1-800-TAX-FORM (1-800-829-3676). Be sure to order using the IRS form or publication number.

A Funny Thing Happened on My Way to Work . . . I Retired

Instructions for Trustees and Issuers

We now provide general and specific form instructions as separate products. The products you should use for 2004 are the **General Instructions for Forms 1099, 1098, 5498, and W-2G** and the **2004 Instructions for Forms 1099-R and 5498.** To order these instructions and additional forms, call 1-800-TAX-FORM (1-800-829-3676).

Caution: *Because paper forms are scanned during processing, you cannot file with the IRS Forms 1096, 1098, 1099, or 5498 that you print from the IRS website.*

Due dates. Furnish Copy B of this form to the participant by May 31, 2005, but furnish fair market value information and RMD if applicable by January 31, 2005.

File Copy A of this form with the IRS by May 31, 2005.

9. Realize that you are not getting any younger and that the day will come when you won't be able to enjoy the things you do today. "Hell begins," Giano-Carlo Menotti has said, "on the day when God grants us a clear vision of all that we have wasted, of all that we might have done, which we did not do. For me," said Menotti, "the conception of hell lies in two words: 'too late.'" I know that I am being very candid here but I want this message to get through to you before it is 'too late.'

Three times Muhammad Ali was the heavyweight-boxing champion of the world, a feat that has never been duplicated. His picture appeared on the cover of *Sports Illustrated* more times than any other athlete. At the height of his popularity he was "floating like a butterfly and stinging like a bee." Everywhere he went reporters, trainers and staff followed him. But that was years ago. Whatever happened to Muhammad Ali? What is he doing today? We saw a cameo appearance at the 2000 Olympic games but where has he been?

A few years ago sportswriter, Gary Smith, went to find out the answer to these questions.

As they were visiting together Ali showed the sportswriter the barn next to his farmhouse. In the barn, on the floor leaning against the walls, were pictures and framed newspaper articles from his prime. There were photos of the champ punching and dancing. There was one picture where his fist was punching the air. There was also a picture of Ali holding his championship

A Funny Thing Happened on My Way to Work . . . I Retired

belt high in triumph. "The Thrilla in Manilla" a framed poster read.

As the sportswriter looked at the pictures he couldn't help but notice they were covered with white streaks; bird droppings. Just then the ex-champ looked into the rafters at the pigeons who made his gym their home. Then perhaps as a statement of despair, Ali walked over to the row of pictures and one by one turned them face down. Then he walked to the door and stared out at the countryside. He mumbled something so low the sportswriter asked him what he said. "I had the world," Muhammed Ali repeated, "and it wasn't nothin.' Look at me now."

(Max Lucado, The Applause of Heaven, Dallas: Word Publishing, 1990, pp. 152–153).

Don't wait for some magical day to pull out all the stops. Enjoying a healthy, common sense income should start the day of retirement. Travel while you can. Catch up on old hobbies and create new ones along the way.

Just the other day, a friend of mine, Weldon Wynn, and I talked. He discovered he has four blocked arteries and he may have diabetes. He told me he spent his whole life working and saving. He has done quite well for himself as a result of honest, hard work. Something he said in our conversation really struck me though. "Steve" he said, "yesterday I went to the farm to feed the cattle. My little granddaughter wanted to go with me, but it was too far to walk so I rode her on the four-wheeler." He went on to say, "We had a wonderful time together. I should have been doing this for years."

Wow! When mortality hits us right in the face we begin to discern what is really important and what is not. How quickly our priorities change in the face of our humanity.

As the Titanic was sinking, a frightened woman found her place in a lifeboat and was about to be lowered into the North Atlantic. Suddenly she thought of something she needed and asked permission to return to her stateroom before they cast off. It was early on, so she was granted three minutes and then they would leave without her.

She ran across the deck that was already slanted at a dangerous angle. She raced through the gambling room with all the money that had rolled to one side. It was ankle deep. She came to her stateroom and quickly pushed aside her diamond rings, her expensive bracelets and necklaces, reached to the shelf above her bed and grabbed three small oranges. Quickly she found her way back to the lifeboat and got in.

Now that seems incredible because thirty minutes earlier she wouldn't have chosen a crate of oranges above one of her smallest diamonds. But death had boarded the Titanic, and one blast of its awful breath had transformed all values. Instantaneously, priceless things had become worthless. Worthless things had become priceless.

CONCLUSION:

In point number two of this chapter I gave you a child's point of view regarding spending and inheritance. Here, I would like to offer a father's perspective. I want nothing more than to give good things to my children. It brings a joy like nothing else when I can be a blessing to my children. Am I contradicting myself here? No, instead, I want to blend this dual relationship into one.

Have you ever flown in a plane? I'm sure you have memorized the safety presentation given by the attendant. I know I do. One interesting caution that the attendant mentions always intrigues me . . . the oxygen masks. They say something like this: "In the unlikely event the cabin would suddenly lose pressure, the oxygen masks will fall down. Blah, blah, blah . . ."if you are traveling with small children, place the mask on *your* face first and then place the mask on the child." Someone has really thought this one out because it makes total sense. The child is helpless and is relying on the adult to care for them. What would happen if the adult tried to save the child by placing the mask on the juvenile first? The adult could pass out before completing the task and both could die. No, it is better for the adult to secure their own air supply first then meet the needs of the child last. In essence, you are better serving your child by taking care of yourself.

As a Father: Do you see where I'm going with this? As a father, if I first take care of myself regarding finances, I will be less likely to need my children's assistance in the event of a financial drought.

As a Child: I really enjoy seeing my mom, who still lives in New Mexico, travel when and where she wants to. I am glad to see my dad, who lives in Missouri, go to his cabin on Black river and fish as much as he wants to.

Find your spending balance and stay with it. Those who truly love you will be glad you made the choice.

"Obstacles are things a person sees when he takes his eyes off his goal."

-Cossman

"For a man to conquer himself is the first and noblest of all virtues."

-Plat

CHAPTER EIGHT

FINDING THE SS MINNOW

SOCIAL SECURITY

You may not know it but many years ago Nikita Kruschev, John F. Kennedy and Golda Meir had a summit meeting with God. Each of them was allowed to ask one question. "God," asked Nikita Kruschev, "do you think the U.S. and Russia will ever have peace?"

"Yes," answered God, "but not in your lifetime."

Then Kennedy spoke. "God, do you think there will be peace between blacks and whites in our land and around the world?"

"Yes," replied God, "but not in your lifetime."

Then it was the Israeli leader's turn. "God," she asked, "do you think there will ever be peace between the Jews and the Arabs?"

"Yes," said God, "but not in *My* lifetime."

Will they ever solve all the ailments of Social Security? Yes, but not in God's lifetime. So . . . just . . .

> "Sit right back and you'll hear a tale,
> a tale of a fateful trip.
> That started from this tropic port
> aboard this tiny ship.
>
> The mate was a mighty sailorman,
> the skipper brave and sure.

Five passengers set sail that day
for a three-hour tour (a three hour tour)."

Is the song stuck in your head now? The latter part of the lyrics is what I want to talk about, so bear with me.

The weather started *getting rough,*
the tiny ship was *tossed.*
If not for the courage of the fearless crew
the Minnow *would be lost.*
    (The Minnow would be lost).
The ship's *aground* on the shore of this uncharted desert isle . . . "

"Ok professor, what is your point?" Take it easy Maryann, and I'll explain. Like the S.S. Minnow, Social Security has been going through some *rough* seas with worker confidence being *tossed* around by what politicians say. Shame on politicians who use fear tactics to elicit votes. Anyway, according to some analysts, if changes aren't made in a few years, Social Security, as we know it, *will be lost.* I want you to carefully read through this chapter. It is my hope that, in so doing, you will discover ways to help reduce the risk of your retirement running *aground.* Although it is unlikely, a catastrophic event regarding Social Security is possible in the future unless sweeping changes are made. It's a long and deep chapter but being the mighty sailor-person you are, you'll do just fine.

Social Security was originally introduced in 1935 in the aftermath of the Great Depression. It was intended to provide a safety net of income to retired and disabled workers and their families. Social Security is a mandatory plan, requiring most wage earners and employers to contribute a percentage of their yearly income to support the program. In return, they, their spouses and sometimes their dependents are eligible for retirement, disability and survivorship benefits. I said "most" are required to contribute. Some individuals who are employed in a religious capacity have the option of "opting out" of paying into social security. Of course, they will not be eligible for federal benefits when they reach retirement age. The reason this "opting out" is available is due to freedom of religion. If a person is employed in a recognized religious capacity, he or she has a limited time period (two years) from his origination date to request being omitted from the required contribution. However, if this person receives wages from any secular income, he must pay Social Security tax on those earnings. A word of caution here for the religious leader who chooses this option: They had better be disciplined enough to invest the amount they would have paid into the Social Security program or else they will put themselves in a dangerous and precarious financial predicament.

The reason I mention this here is because there has been talk among politicians regarding the privatization of Social Security. Both sides are staunch opponents of the opposing side. I can see merits in both camps but the primary ingredient would need to be self-discipline. Without this willpower, a private Social Security plan would prove disastrous.

Today, over 92% of the people over 65 receive a Social Security benefit check. For many this monthly benefit represents their main source of retirement income. As I mentioned, it is for this very reason that I sat down to write this book. (Remember my door-knocking discovery in chapter one).

Every year you work (or worked), you and your employer contribute equal amounts to Social Security, as required by the Federal Insurance Contribution Act (FICA). In 2004, 6.2% of your earned income was withheld from your paycheck to fund Social Security. Another 1.45% went to Medicare for a total deduction of 7.65%. Your employer matched your contributions with an additional 7.65% of your earnings going into the programs mentioned. If you are self-employed, you have the privilege of paying the entire 15.3% yourself, hence the reason some

A Funny Thing Happened on My Way to Work . . . I Retired

religious leaders choose to opt out. This tax is in addition to state and federal income tax. Whew!

When you get a Social Security card, your Social Security benefit account is opened. It is not activated until you begin earning income. Once your earnings begin, the amount you contribute each year is recorded.

The accuracy of this record is important. You can get a copy of your earnings record from the Social Security Administration (SSA). Fill out Form 7004 and mail it to SSA. The forms are available at your local Social Security office or by calling 800–772–1213. If you discover your record is wrong, you can ask that it be corrected, though you must supply evidence of errors. The SSA encourages people to check their earnings records every three years or so, since the earlier a problem is found, the easier it is to prove and correct.

Did you know?

- 17% of the country's population receives Social Security benefits
- The majority get retirement money
- 92% of the people over age 65 receive benefits
- Almost 70% of the people applying for retirement benefits each year are under 65
- Social Security paid over $585 billion in benefits in 1998

OTHER FACTS YOU SHOULD KNOW ABOUT SOCIAL SECURITY:

1. Social Security *disability* benefits do not continue past Normal Retirement Age. Retirement benefits must then be applied for and replace disability benefits. No double dipping allowed.
2. There is a limit to the amount of benefits that can be paid on each Social Security record called the Maximum

Family Benefit, generally around 150 to 180 percent of the worker's benefit. If this limit is exceeded, the family benefits are reduced.
3. Ex-spouses, widows and divorced widows may all be eligible for benefits on a spouse's record. Provided the requirements are met, they may even all be collecting on the same worker's record. This is extremely important information to understand. I have several clients whose spouses died *after* they were divorced. Some found, to their delight, that they were entitled to Social Security income derived from the deceased, ex-spouse. Be sure to check this out completely.
4. There are two Social Security trust funds: one used to finance retirement and survivor's benefits and the other used to finance the disability program. Money not used to pay current benefits is invested only in U. S. Government Treasury bonds. Although this type of financial security allows for maximum safety, it provides a less than stellar return in the form of interest. (Refer back to our "CD Real Rate of Return" chart).
5. Social Security benefits do not automatically start coming in the mail the first day of Normal Retirement Age. ***They must be applied for!*** The easiest way is to set up an appointment with the local Social Security office or call 1-800-772-1213.
6. As I mentioned earlier, to get an official statement of all the earnings recorded in your Social Security account, an estimate of your current disability and death benefits, and an estimate of future retirement benefits, fill out Form #7004 Request for Earnings & Benefit Estimate Statement.

Form Approved
OMB No. 0960-0466 ☐ SP

Request for *Social Security Statement*

☐ Please check this box if you want to get your *Statement* in Spanish instead of English.

Please print or type your answers. When you have completed the form, fold it and mail it to us. (If you prefer to send your request using the Internet, contact us at *www.socialsecurity.gov*)

1. Name shown on your Social Security card:

   ______________ First Name ______ Middle Initial

   ______________ Last Name Only

2. Your Social Security number as shown on your card:

   ☐☐☐ - ☐☐ - ☐☐☐☐

3. Your date of birth (Mo.-Day-Yr.)

   ☐☐ - ☐☐ - ☐☐☐☐

4. Other Social Security numbers you have used:

   ☐☐☐ - ☐☐ - ☐☐☐☐

   ☐☐☐ - ☐☐ - ☐☐☐☐

5. Your Sex: ☐ Male ☐ Female

For items 6 and 8 show only earnings covered by Social Security. Do NOT include wages from state, local or federal government employment that are NOT covered for Social Security or that are covered ONLY by Medicare.

6. Show your actual earnings (wages and/or net self-employment income) for last year and your estimated earnings for this year.

   A. Last year's actual earnings: *(Dollars Only)*

   $☐☐☐,☐☐☐.00

   B. This year's estimated earnings: *(Dollars Only)*

   $☐☐☐,☐☐☐.00

7. Show the age at which you plan to stop working.

   ☐☐ *(Show only one age)*

8. Below, show the average yearly amount (not your total future lifetime earnings) that you think you will earn between now and when you plan to stop working. Include performance or scheduled pay increases or bonuses, but not cost-of-living increases.

   If you expect to earn significantly more or less in the future due to promotions, job changes, part-time work, or an absence from the work force, enter the amount that most closely reflects your future average yearly earnings.

   If you don't expect any significant changes, show the same amount you are earning now (the amount in 6B).

   Future average yearly earnings: *(Dollars Only)*

   $☐☐☐,☐☐☐.00

9. Do you want us to send the *Statement:*
   - To you? Enter your name and mailing address.
   - To someone else (your accountant, pension plan, etc.)? Enter your name with "c/o" and the name and address of that person or organization.

   ______________ "C/O" or Street Address (Include Apt. No., P.O. Box, Rural Route)

   ______________ Street Address

   ______________ Street Address (If Foreign Address, enter City, Province, Postal Code)

   ______________ U.S. City, State, Zip code (If Foreign Address, enter Name of Country only)

NOTICE:
I am asking for information about my own Social Security record or the record of a person I am authorized to represent. I declare under penalty of perjury that I have examined all the information on this form, and on any accompanying statements or forms, and it is true and correct to the best of my knowledge. I authorize you to use a contractor to send the *Social Security Statement* to the person and address in item 9.

▶

Please sign your name (Do Not Print)

Date (Area Code) Daytime Telephone No.

Form **SSA-7004-SM** (1-2003) EF (01-2003)
Destroy prior editions

You can mail these forms to:

Social Security Administration
Wilkes Barre Data Operations Center
P.O. Box 7004
Wilkes Barre, PA 18767–7004

7. If you do not find and correct errors in your Social Security record within 3 years, they become part of your permanent record. Therefore, you might want to check on them every 3 years or so. If you find any errors, submit form 7008.

Steve Kiefer

SOCIAL SECURITY ADMINISTRATION

Form Approved
OMB NO. 0960-0029

REQUEST FOR CORRECTION OF EARNINGS RECORD

Paperwork/Privacy Act Notice: The information requested on this form is authorized by section 205(c)(4) and (5) of the Social Security Act. This information is collected to resolve any discrepancy on your earnings record. The information you provide will be used to correct your earnings record where any discrepancy exists. Your response to this request is voluntary; however, failure to provide all or part of the requested information may affect your future eligibility for benefits and the amounts of benefits to which you may become entitled. Information furnished on this form may be disclosed by the Social Security Administration to another person or governmental agency only with respect to Social Security programs to comply with Federal laws requiring the exchange of information between the Social Security Administration and another agency.

I have examined your statement (or record) of my Social Security earnings and it is not correct. I am providing the following information and accompanying evidence so that you can correct my record.

1. Print your name (First Name, Middle Initial, Last Name)	2. Enter your date of birth (Month, Day, Year)

3. Print your name as shown on your Social Security number card

4. Print any other name used in your work. (If you have used no other name enter "None.")

5. (a) Enter your Social Security number __ __ __ / __ __ / __ __ __ __	5. (b) Enter any other Social Security number(s) used by you or your employer to report your wages or self-employment. If none, check, "None."
	(1) ☐ None
	(2) __ __ __ / __ __ / __ __ __ __
	(3) __ __ __ / __ __ / __ __ __ __

6. IF NECESSARY, SSA MAY DISCLOSE MY NAME TO MY EMPLOYERS: ⟶ ☐ YES ☐ NO
(Without permission to use your name, SSA cannot make a thorough investigation.)

⟶ If you disagree with wages reported to your earnings record, complete Item 7.
⟶ If you disagree with self-employment income recorded on your earnings record, go to Item 8.

7. Print below in date order your employment **only** for year(s) (or months) you believe our records are not correct. If you need more space, attach a separate sheet. Please make only one entry per calendar period employed. Show quarterly wage periods and amounts for years prior to 1978; annual amounts, 1978 on.

1 - Year(s) (or months) of employment 2 - Type of employment (e.g., agricultural)	Employer's business name, address, and phone number *(include number, city, state, and zip code)*	My correct Social Security (FICA) wages were:	My evidence of my correct earnings (enclosed)
(a) 1. 2.			__ W2 or W-2C __ Other (Specify)
(b) 1. 2.			__ W2 or W-2C __ Other (Specify)
(c) 1. 2.			__ W2 or W-2C __ Other (Specify)

⟶ If you do not have evidence of these earnings, you must explain why you are unable to submit such evidence in the remarks section of Item 10.
⟶ If you do not have self-employment income that is incorrect go on to item 10 for any remarks, and then complete Item 11.

8. Print below in date order your self-employment earnings only for years you believe our records are not correct. Please make only one entry per year.

Trade or business name and business address	Year(s) of self-employment	My correct self-employment earnings were:
		$
		$

FORM **SSA-7008** (5-1988) EF (12-2001)   (over)

187

8. You can work during retirement, but if you earn too much it will reduce the size of the benefits you are receiving from age 62 up to age 65. The limits on such earnings are currently $11,280. Benefits are reduced by $1 for every $2 that you earn over this amount. You can work after age 65 as much as you want with benefits unreduced, although they may become taxable if you earn too much.
9. You can increase the size of your retirement benefit by delaying collecting and remaining on the job past full retirement age. This higher benefit comes from extra earnings toward your account and a credit awarded for this patience, ranging from 3% to 8% of your benefit depending on your date of birth.

I know that was a long walk but this information can be very useful to you in determining your retirement income. You might even find a pleasant surprise regarding Social Security for a change.

Most financial advisors say you'll need about 70 percent of your pre-retirement earnings to comfortably maintain your pre-retirement standard of living. Under current law, if you have average earnings, your Social Security retirement benefits will replace only about 38 percent, so you'll need to supplement your benefits with a pension from your former employer, from personal savings or from investments. Ideally, having all three as a source is the most desirable position.

Social Security is a compact between generations. For more than 65 years, America has kept the promise of security for its workers and their families. But now, the Social Security system is facing serious future financial problems, and action is needed soon to make sure the system is sound when today's younger workers are ready for retirement.

Today there are almost 36 million Americans age 65 or older. The Social Security of these senior's retirement benefits are funded by today's workers and their employers who jointly pay Social Security taxes—just as the money they paid into Social Security was used to pay benefits to those who retired before them.

Unless action is taken soon to strengthen Social Security, it is estimated that in just 14 years we will begin paying more in benefits than we collect in taxes! Further estimates conclude that without changes, by 2042 the Social Security Trust Fund will be exhausted. By then, the number of Americans 65 or older is expected to have doubled. There won't be enough younger people working to pay all of the benefits owed to those who are retiring. At that point, there will be enough money to pay only about 73 cents for each dollar of scheduled benefits. We will need to resolve these issues soon to make sure Social Security continues to provide a foundation of protection for future generations as it has done in the past.

I wish I could offer better news or at least better solutions to this pending dilemma, but my best advice is to plan for the worst. Let's continue.

TWELVE OF THE MOST IMPORTANT QUESTIONS ABOUT SOCIAL SECURITY

Below are twelve questions designed to probe into less familiar areas of the Social Security maze. Unfortunately it is not an exhaustive list, BUT I have provided various links for further study. As always, call my office if you need to be pointed in the right direction.

1. **Where Can I Go to Find Answers to Questions About Social Security Benefits?**

As I mentioned, my intent for this section is to give you some basic information regarding Social Security and your retirement. For further study, go to www.ssa.gov or call your local Social Security Office.

A Funny Thing Happened on My Way to Work . . . I Retired

2. **What is the maximum Social Security benefit I can be paid if I retire this year at age 65?**

   A worker retiring (in 2005) at age 66 and eleven months, who also made $80,000 in the previous year could receive about $1,780 per month. Of course this depends on past contributions to the system. *Source:* Social Security Administration.

3. **What's the best way to get an accurate estimate of my Social Security Benefits?**

   Request a "Personal Earnings and Benefit Estimate Statement" form from the Social Security office, complete and send it in, and you will receive a record of your wage history and an estimated retirement benefits statement. You can also request a Social Security Statement through the Internet at the home website www.ssa.gov.

4. **When should I file for my Social Security and what documents will I need?**

   Normally, most advisors recommend you file for Social Security three months before you plan to receive benefits. However, I would begin the process at least six months prior to the exit date. As the "boomers" get closer, it may take more time to process the potential influx of paperwork. Here is what you will need:

   1. *Your Social Security card.* Not a copy or one made in a machine. Those look good but will not be accepted. If you lost your card or if it was destroyed, you can obtain a new one through your local post office. Even if you are not yet ready to retire, be sure to have this card handy.
   2. *Proof of your age.* (I have to tell this story here). When my aunt was ready to retire she went to the local Social Security administration office in Indiana to file the appropriate documents. When it came time

for her to give proof of her age, she gave the administration officer her birth date. Unfortunately, the month she gave, which was the same month she had used to celebrate her birthday for 65 years, didn't match her newly printed birth certificate she had acquired from the hospital earlier that day. Apparently, Grandma, God rest her soul, made a "mistake" when she celebrated my aunts first birthday. She should have been celebrating two months earlier. Oops! Why am I airing my families "dirty laundry" here? In hopes that you will have all of your ducks in a row when the time comes to retire and avoid any unpleasant, shall we say, "surprises." Don't tell my mom I put this story in my book. I mean it.

3. *Tax forms from the previous year.* It would be a good idea to bring in returns from three years prior just in case.
4. *Marriage certificate/divorce documents, if any.* These must be originals. A word of advice for divorcees: keep your marriage license in a safe place even if the divorce was ugly. In case the ex-spouse dies, you will need it in order to apply for a larger monthly Social Security check.
5. *Death Certificate, if applying for survivor benefits.* If you are divorced and your ex-spouse dies while married to someone else, you may have to wait until you are 65 to draw any benefits from them. If not, you may be able to draw as early as 62. Find out.

(*For a complete list of documents you will need at retirement, see chapter eleven*).

5. **How much income can I earn from employment without affecting Social Security payments?**
This is an important question to be answered since many

retirees move from fulltime employment into a part time setting.

According to the Social Security Administration, Individuals under age 65 can earn up to $11,280 with a reduction of $1 in benefits for every $2 earned *over* the $11,280 limit.

Social Security recipients 65 and older no longer have earning limits.

6. **The next logical question is will my Social Security be taxed?**

This is a confusing subject for many retirees who don't understand the tax issues of earnings as they relate to Social Security. The question is: "Am I through with the IRS?"

A prominent citizen of Washington D. C. once invited President John F. Kennedy to play golf when Kennedy was President. On the first hole Kennedy floated a nice shot about three feet from the pin. He walked up to the ball and glanced over at the man who had invited him. Kennedy was looking for the man to concede him the putt. The man ignored him, and stared up at the sky.

"You're certainly going to give me this putt, aren't you?" Kennedy asked.

"Make a pass at it," the man replied. "I want to see your stroke. A putt like that builds character. Besides, it will give you a little feel for the greens."

With an anguished look, Kennedy said, "I work in the Oval Office all day for citizens like you," he said. "And now you're not going to give me this putt?" The man said nothing. "O.K," Kennedy sighed. "But let's keep moving. I've got an appointment after we finish with the director of Internal Revenue."

The man quickly said, "The putt is good," and moved on.

It just goes to show, you can't escape the IRS even on the golf course.

Before I go any further, I want to clarify what the IRS interprets "income" to be. Basically there are two types of income, earned and unearned.

Earned income:

Earned income is derived from wages earned as a result of employment both before and after retirement. Any income you bring home from a job, whether it is from taking orders at McDonalds or from greeting services performed for Wal-Mart, it is considered earned income. Wages = earned income.

Unearned income:

This sounds like an oxymoron. How can I receive an income for something I did not earn? The term simply refers to any income from something other than wages, i.e. interest from savings, CDs, or other investment sources. Rental income is also considered unearned income.

Be sure you calculate what your entire income will be prior to retirement or you might end up with unexpected taxes.

Here's how it works. Following is the formula used to determine your provisional income.

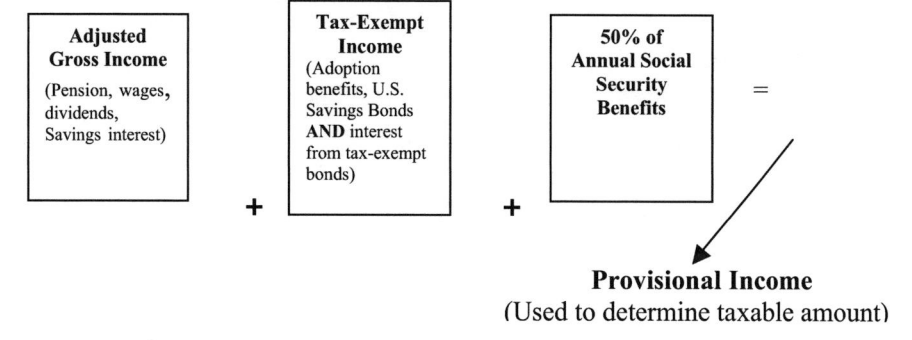

| Adjusted Gross Income (Pension, wages, dividends, Savings interest) | + | Tax-Exempt Income (Adoption benefits, U.S. Savings Bonds AND interest from tax-exempt bonds) | + | 50% of Annual Social Security Benefits | = |

Provisional Income
(Used to determine taxable amount)

The key to estimating your potential tax liability on your social security benefits is the *provisional* income figure.

Now, back to the original question regarding Social Security and taxes.

*For couples filing a **joint** tax return:*
>If your provisional income (see above) is less than $32,000, your benefits are not taxable. Between $32,000 and $44,000, up to 50% of your Social Security may be included as taxable income. If your provisional income is over $44,000, up to 85% of your Social Security benefits can be exposed to income taxes. Currently 85% is the maximum amount of Social Security that will be taxed regardless of the income. In other words, you can make a gazillion dollars after age 65 and the maximum amount of your social security benefits that can be taxed is 85%.

*For **single** taxpayers:*
>If your provisional income is less than $25,000, your benefits are not taxable. Between $25,000 and $34,000, up to 50% of Social Security can be included in taxable income. Provisional income that exceeds $34,000, can cause up to 85% of your Social Security benefits to be taxed.

Since we have been dealing with general numbers up to this point, let me show you how to figure the taxable amount of your social security benefits. Let's do an exercise:

Tarzan and Jane are retired from the jungle. Together they bring in a combined income of $38,700. Their combined Social Security income is $18,500.

Since their provisional income (see provisional chart above) exceeds the base amount of $32,000, (38,700 + 9,250 = 47,950) a portion of their social security check will likely be taxable. The question is, how much?

Steve Kiefer

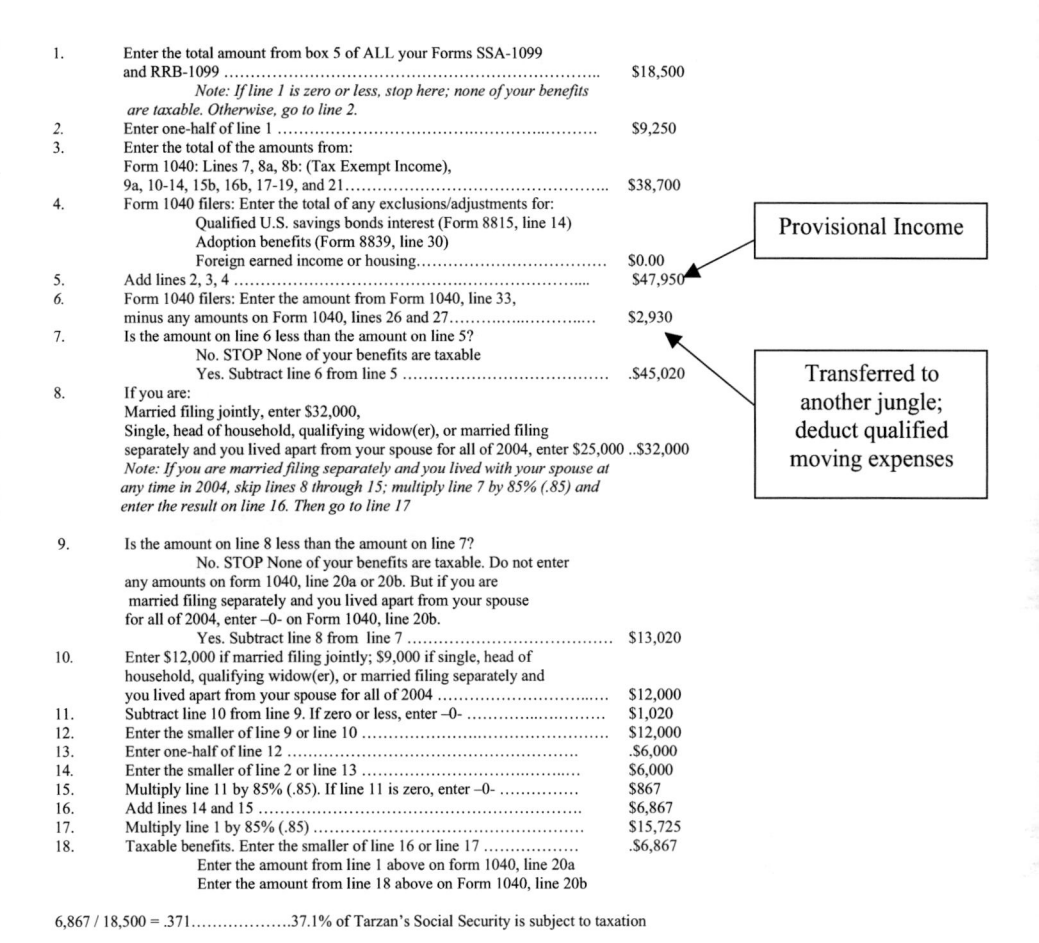

1.	Enter the total amount from box 5 of ALL your Forms SSA-1099 and RRB-1099	$18,500
	Note: If line 1 is zero or less, stop here; none of your benefits are taxable. Otherwise, go to line 2.	
2.	Enter one-half of line 1	$9,250
3.	Enter the total of the amounts from: Form 1040: Lines 7, 8a, 8b: (Tax Exempt Income), 9a, 10-14, 15b, 16b, 17-19, and 21.................................	$38,700
4.	Form 1040 filers: Enter the total of any exclusions/adjustments for: Qualified U.S. savings bonds interest (Form 8815, line 14) Adoption benefits (Form 8839, line 30) Foreign earned income or housing..................................	$0.00
5.	Add lines 2, 3, 4	$47,950
6.	Form 1040 filers: Enter the amount from Form 1040, line 33, minus any amounts on Form 1040, lines 26 and 27......................	$2,930
7.	Is the amount on line 6 less than the amount on line 5? No. STOP None of your benefits are taxable Yes. Subtract line 6 from line 5	.$45,020
8.	If you are: Married filing jointly, enter $32,000, Single, head of household, qualifying widow(er), or married filing separately and you lived apart from your spouse for all of 2004, enter $25,000 ..$32,000 *Note: If you are married filing separately and you lived with your spouse at any time in 2004, skip lines 8 through 15; multiply line 7 by 85% (.85) and enter the result on line 16. Then go to line 17*	
9.	Is the amount on line 8 less than the amount on line 7? No. STOP None of your benefits are taxable. Do not enter any amounts on form 1040, line 20a or 20b. But if you are married filing separately and you lived apart from your spouse for all of 2004, enter –0– on Form 1040, line 20b. Yes. Subtract line 8 from line 7	$13,020
10.	Enter $12,000 if married filing jointly; $9,000 if single, head of household, qualifying widow(er), or married filing separately and you lived apart from your spouse for all of 2004	$12,000
11.	Subtract line 10 from line 9. If zero or less, enter –0–	$1,020
12.	Enter the smaller of line 9 or line 10	$12,000
13.	Enter one-half of line 12	.$6,000
14.	Enter the smaller of line 2 or line 13	$6,000
15.	Multiply line 11 by 85% (.85). If line 11 is zero, enter –0–	$867
16.	Add lines 14 and 15	$6,867
17.	Multiply line 1 by 85% (.85)	$15,725
18.	Taxable benefits. Enter the smaller of line 16 or line 17	.$6,867
	Enter the amount from line 1 above on form 1040, line 20a Enter the amount from line 18 above on Form 1040, line 20b	

6,867 / 18,500 = .371....................37.1% of Tarzan's Social Security is subject to taxation

[Provisional Income — arrow pointing to line 5]

[Transferred to another jungle; deduct qualified moving expenses — arrow pointing to line 6]

Tarzan and Jane will have to show $6,867 of their $18,500 as taxable income. Obviously this is not 85 percent of their benefits. What percentage is it? To find out we take the taxable amount (6867) and divide it by the total amount received (18500). 6867/18500 = .37. So, 37.1 percent of Tarzan's Social Security is subject to taxation. As provisional income goes up, so does the amount of social security funds subject to tax.

Keep this important fact in mind however; this amount ($6,867) is added to other income on page one of form 1040. If you have enough itemized deductions to draw your adjusted

A Funny Thing Happened on My Way to Work . . . I Retired

gross income down to zero, you won't have to pay any tax on your social security. Talk to a tax professional when dealing with this subject.

I've included a blank worksheet for you to fill out when you are ready to retire so you can get an idea of what is coming.

Steve Kiefer

Worksheet to determine amount of taxable Social Security

1. Enter the total amount from box 5 of ALL your Forms SSA-1099 and RRB-1099 .... _____
   Note: If line 1 is zero or less, stop here; none of your benefits are taxable. Otherwise, go to line 2.
2. Enter one-half of line 1 .... _____
3. Enter the total of the amounts from:
   Form 1040: Lines 7, 8a, 8b: (Tax Exempt Income),
   9a, 10-14, 15b, 16b, 17-19, and 21.................................... _____
4. Form 1040 filers: Enter the total of any exclusions/adjustments for:
       Qualified U.S. savings bonds interest (Form 8815, line 14)
       Adoption benefits (Form 8839, line 30)
       Foreign earned income or housing............................ _____
5. Add lines 2, 3, 4 .... _____
6. Form 1040 filers: Enter the amount from Form 1040, line 33, minus any amounts on Form 1040, lines 26 and 27................... _____
7. Is the amount on line 6 less than the amount on line 5?
       No. STOP None of your benefits are taxable
       Yes. Subtract line 6 from line 5 .... _____
8. If you are:
   Married filing jointly, enter $32,000, Single, head of household, qualifying widow(er), or married filing separately and you lived apart from your spouse for all of 2004, enter $25,000...... _____
   Note: If you are married filing separately and you lived with your spouse at any time in 2004, skip lines 8 through 15; multiply line 7 by 85% (.85) and enter the result on line 16. Then go to line 17
9. Is the amount on line 8 less than the amount on line 7?
       No. STOP None of your benefits are taxable. Do not enter any amounts on form 1040, line 20a or 20b. But if you are married filing separately and you lived apart from your spouse for all of 2004, enter –0- on Form 1040, line 20b.
       Yes. Subtract line 8 from line 7 .... _____
10. Enter $12,000 if married filing jointly; $9,000 if single, head of household, qualifying widow(er), or married filing separately and you lived apart from your spouse for all of 2004 .... _____
11. Subtract line 10 from line 9. If zero or less, enter –0- .... _____
12. Enter the smaller of line 9 or line 10 .... _____
13. Enter one-half of line 12 .... _____
14. Enter the smaller of line 2 or line 13 .... _____
15. Multiply line 11 by 85% (.85). If line 11 is zero, enter –0- .... _____
16. Add lines 14 and 15 .... _____
17. Multiply line 1 by 85% (.85) .... _____
18. Taxable benefits. Enter the smaller of line 16 or line 17 .... _____
        Enter the amount from line 1 above on form 1040, line 20a
        Enter the amount from line 18 above on Form 1040, line 20b

A Funny Thing Happened on My Way to Work . . . I Retired

7. **Should I file for Social Security early if I decide to retire before my normal retirement age? If so, what is the reduction?**

Retiring before age 65 can be a rewarding experience. Being able to finally do the things you've dreamed of and being healthy enough to still enjoy them is priceless. However, there is a cost to consider before taking early retirement.

For individuals born in 1937 and before, normal retirement (the age at which a recipient is entitled to 100% of his or her Social Security Income benefit) is 65 years of age. For each month you choose to collect social security income before the "normal" retirement age, your payment is reduced by .555%. The earliest you can collect is age 62 and the benefits would be 80% of your "normal" Social Security Income.

For individuals born after 1937 the reduced benefit is 79.17% at age 62, and the normal retirement age increases from 65 and two months to 67 years of age, depending on the year of birth.

The complete table of Social Security Full Retirement and Reduction by Age can be found at www.ssa.gov/retirechartred.html. *Source:* Social Security Administration.

Attaining full Social Security retirement age is evolving. Below is the latest chart.

Year of Birth	Full Retirement Age
37	65
38	65 and 2 months
39	65 and 4 months
40	65 and 6 months
41	65 and 8 months
42	65 and 10 months
43-54	66
55	66 and 2 months
56	66 and 4 months
57	66 and 6 months
58	66 and 8 months
59	66 and 10 months
60	67

If you were born on January 1st of any year you should refer to the previous year.

8. Are my benefits figured on my last five years of earnings?

No. Retirement benefit calculations are based on your average earnings during a lifetime of work under the Social Security system. For most current and future retirees, your average will be based on your 35 highest years of earnings. Years in which you have low earnings or no earnings may be counted to bring the total years of earnings up to 35.

9. I stopped work at the end of last year at age 52. I don't expect to work again before I start my Social

Security benefits when I turn 62. Will I still get the same benefit amount as if I retired at age 62?

The answer is, probably not. Normally, when an average is done to calculate your benefit, it is based on your highest 35 years of earnings. The assumption in the calculation is you would continue to work up to age 62, making the same earnings you made last year. If, instead, you have $0 earnings each year over the next 10 years, your average earnings will probably be less and so will your benefit. You can use a *detailed* benefit calculator to see how this will affect your monthly benefit amount.

10. **Will my pension reduce the amount of my Social Security benefit?**

If your pension is from work where you also paid in Social Security taxes, it will not affect your Social Security benefit. However, a pension based on work that is not covered by Social Security (for example, the federal civil service and some state, local, or foreign government systems) will most likely reduce the amount of your Social Security benefit.

11. **My wife and I both worked under Social Security. Her Social Security Statement says she can get $850 a month at full retirement age and mine says I would get $1450. Do we each get our own amount? Someone told me we could get my full amount, but only one-half of my wife's amount. Is this true?**

Fortunately, the answer is no. Since your wife's benefit amount is more than one-half of *your* benefit amount, you will each get your full benefit. If your wife's own benefit were less than half of yours (in this hypothetical case, less than $725), she would receive her amount plus enough on your record to bring it up to the $725 amount.

Example I: Joe is eligible to receive a monthly Social Security check in the amount of $1,300. Joe's wife, Jane is eligible for only $600 per month. Since $600 is less than half of

Joe's $1,300, the monthly income will be enhanced by $50 to bring Jane's check up to $650.

Example 2: Pete is getting a Social Security check for $1,400 per month. His wife, Pam, who worked in a high-income trade, is eligible for a $1,350 benefit check. Since Pam's check is more than half of her husbands, they both will receive their full payout benefit.

12. If I work after I start receiving Social Security retirement benefits, will I still have to pay Social Security and Medicare taxes on my earnings?

Unfortunately, the answer is yes. Any time you work in a job that is covered by Social Security, even if you are already receiving Social Security benefits, you and your employer must pay the Social Security and Medicare taxes on your earnings. The same is true if you are self-employed; you are still subject to the Social Security and Medicare taxes on your net profit.

A sportswriter once asked Joe Louis, "Who hit you the hardest during your ring career?" His reply was "Uncle Sam."

Being retired doesn't mean you are out of the "ring" with Uncle Sam so be sure to factor in all the tax consequences of going back to work.

13. Someone told me that Social Security has a financial planning service. I don't understand the connection between financial planning and Social Security.

Social Security is not in the financial planning business. However, Social Security can offer you a free Social Security Statement to help you in assessing your financial planning needs. The statement gives you a breakdown of all the wages reported under your social security number as well as estimates of what Social Security benefits you and your family would be eligible for.

Let me stress the importance of seeking professional

help to accomplish this task. (See the *Picking the Right Captain* chapter).

Once you know what to expect from Social Security, you can plan your other financial needs. I encourage you to visit the Ball Park Estimate calculator of the American Savings Education Council and study your other retirement income options, and FirstGov for Seniors to learn more about retirement planning. www.firstgov.org They offer comprehensive information on savings, investments, pensions, medical insurance, and housing. They also offer a senior's retirement planner on their website.

Some people who get Social Security benefits have to pay income tax on a portion of those benefits. This will apply to you only if you have other substantial income such as wages, self-employment income, interest, dividends and other taxable income that you have to report on your tax return. Even interest earned on tax-free investments such as municipal bonds are included in this figure. Finally, one half of your social security benefits will be included making up your *provisional income* figure. No one pays taxes on more than 85 percent of his or her Social Security benefits and some pay on a smaller amount, based on these IRS rules:

- ◆ **If you are married but file a separate tax return**, AND you lived together for any portion of the previous tax year, you probably will pay taxes on your Social Security benefits.

REMEMBER . . .

***On your 1040 tax return, your *"provisional income"* is the sum of your adjusted gross income plus nontaxable interest plus one-half of your Social Security benefits.**

Every January you will receive a Social Security Benefit Statement (Form SSA-1099) showing the amount of benefits you received in the previous year.

Steve Kiefer

FORM SSA-1099 – SOCIAL SECURITY BENEFIT STATEMENT	
2004 • PART OF YOUR SOCIAL SECURITY BENEFITS SHOWN IN BOX 5 MAY BE TAXABLE INCOME. • SEE THE REVERSE FOR MORE INFORMATION.	
Box 1. Name	Box 2. Beneficiary's Social Security Number
Box 3. Benefits Paid in 2004 / Box 4. Benefits Repaid to SSA in 2004	Box 5. Net Benefits for 2004 (Box 3 minus Box 4)
DESCRIPTION OF AMOUNT IN BOX 3	DESCRIPTION OF AMOUNT IN BOX 4
	Box 6. Voluntary Federal Income Tax Withholding
	Box 7. Address
	Box 8. Claim Number (Use this number if you need to contact SSA)
Form SSA-1099-SM (1-2005) DO NOT RETURN THIS FORM TO SSA OR IRS	

You can use this statement when you complete your federal income tax return to find out if your benefits are subject to tax. (See worksheet above).

Although you're not required to have federal taxes withheld from your Social Security benefits, you may find it easier than paying quarterly estimated tax payments

> *"Character is who you are when no one but GOD is looking."*
>
> -Andy Dukes

CHAPTER NINE

PICKING THE RIGHT CAPTAIN

A Bridgeport Connecticut telegram was sent after a major catastrophe that read, "So far the death toll is officially estimated at 5,000 but is expected to rise as help reaches outlying towns."

That sounds like the kind of help we don't need. Some feel the same way about a financial advisor. "I don't need his help to lose my money. I can do it just fine on my own."

I'm amused at the TV commercials that try to depict Financial Advisors as warm touchy-feely people while they're dressed like a funeral director in an office with 50 cubicles surrounding them. I'm not saying that appearance constitutes merit or demerit when choosing a broker, but it is wise to go deeper in your investigation than merely choosing a company based on its popularity. CHOOSE YOUR CAPTAIN (ADVISOR) BECAUSE OF WHO HE OR SHE IS AND BECAUSE HE OR SHE SHARES AN INVESTMENT PHILOSOPHY THAT MATCHES YOURS.

The other day one of my clients called and wanted me to pull them out of their holdings, as they put it: "When you see the market trends moving down." This account is worth about $700,000 with about $100,000 in gains. After the client persisted *ad nauseam,* I finally told him he needed to find another broker; one that would be willing to time the market because that was not my philosophy . . . he stayed with me and is up another $30,000+.

A Funny Thing Happened on My Way to Work . . . I Retired

BELOW IS A LIST OF WHAT MOST CLIENTS SAY THEY WANT IN A CLIENT/BROKER RELATIONSHIP.

1. Trust: People view their relationship with their Advisor as a counselor
2. Contact: Clients want frequent contact and quality personal service from Advisors
3. Performance: Clients want reasonable investment performance
4. Direction: A written financial plan is often desired
5. Experience: A knowledgeable, competent Advisor is required to provide timely customized advice.
6. Reduce Risk: Most clients need a plan that becomes more conservative with time, especially during the retirement years. A rule of thumb: Base your risk tolerance on the amount of time you have before the event. (See example)

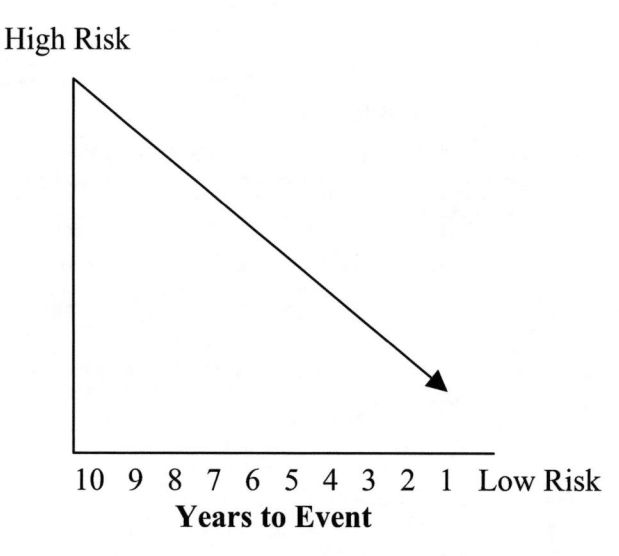

High Risk

10 9 8 7 6 5 4 3 2 1   Low Risk
Years to Event

As you can see in this diagram, risk is in direct relation to time. The less time you have to recover from potential loss, the more conservative your investment suitability should be. I remember a couple coming into my office a few years ago and telling me their son was two years away from college. They wanted me to put some college money they had saved into something that would offer the fastest growth over the two-year period. I shared with them that such a strategy was not in their best interest. Yes, they needed as much growth as possible, but in the context of time verse risk. The less time you have to save for an event, the more conservative you should be.

7. Taxes: Tax reduction plans should always be addressed at any level of the investment process but especially after retirement.
8. Family: Clients look for an Advisor who has a genuine concern for their (the client's) family and children. Simple planning steps taken now can greatly reduce taxes and anxiety when the time comes to transfer wealth. (Much more on the subject of wills and trusts in Chapter eleven).
9. Retirement: Most clients are not seeking to get rich as much as they are trying to build for a comfortable retirement. Having enough to retire on is what most individuals want and need.
10. Simplicity: :*Adjusting for the beta of a stock's long-term outlook as it relates to the P.E. ratio. . . .*" Sounds impressive but it makes no sense to the average investor. Look for an Advisor who uses layman's terms to describe the investment recommendations. You NEED to know where your money is and what it is doing. Remember, buy and hold does NOT mean buy and forget.

In spite of the obvious need to seek professional help to assist in managing your money, people still insist on doing it themselves. I have compiled a list of the top ten reasons why people choose to invest on their *own* rather than use a professional. (Drum roll, please).

REASON NUMBER 10: "I do not believe in paying *anyone* for his or her expertise"

In addition to managing my own portfolio, I also diagnosed and removed my Uncle Bubba's ruptured appendix. He's fine and according to the Internet, the infection should go away soon. I always trust what's on the Internet. By the way, would you like me to perform lipo-suction on you for free?

REASON NUMBER 9: "For nighttime reading, I enjoy a warm fire and a 3000 page mutual fund prospectus"

In fact, if I read five prospectuses a day for the next two decades, I might just put a dent in the 8,000+ funds out there. Who needs good communication in marriage anyway? It's funny though how sunlight now hurts my eyes.

REASON NUMBER 8: "I'm the only person alive with a real working crystal ball"

A self-invested retiree was fishing in a lake and caught a strange fish. He had never seen one quite like it before. Suddenly the fish spoke to the man.

"Please throw me back in the lake," begged the fish, "and I'll grant you three wishes."

The retiree considered the request and replied, "make it five and we've got a deal."

"I can grant only three," gasped the fish.

"Four and a half," the man suggested.

"Three," the fish replied faintly.

"Okay, okay, three it is," the retiree conceded.

The fish did not reply. It lay dead on the bottom of the boat.

Even if a crystal ball can see the future, who can stop greed? One important job of your financial advisor is to help you take emotion out of investing. Save emotional attachments for relationships, it has *no* place in your financial portfolio.

Chuck Swindoll says that in the Marines he was taught

to dig a hole big enough for two men when preparing for combat. There's nothing quite like fighting a battle all alone. There's something strengthening about having a buddy with you who can keep you from panicking. Don't make the mistake of fighting your investment battles alone. You might panic and jump out at the wrong time.

REASON NUMBER 7: "I have nerves of steel - I never get spooked in bear markets"

After Santa Anna defeated the Texas force at the Alamo, he pursued the troops under the command of Sam Houston. Houston's badly outnumbered force was backed against the San Jacinto River. Cut off by the superior numbers of Santa Anna, Houston made his final battle plan. While doing so, he called his faithful orderly and close friend "Deaf" Smith and commanded him to burn the bridge behind them, which crossed the San Jacinto River. Smith responded by reminding Houston that the bridge was the only way out, the only route of retreat. Houston replied, "Burn the bridge. That's not the way we are going out of here." Smith burned the bridge. Soon thereafter, Houston gave the command that resulted in the total defeat of the Mexican army.

Sam Houston was a man that truly could have been a self-investor. Do you have nerves of steel like this? "For your information, Steve, the 508-point market crash in 1987 didn't bother me a bit. And these last three years have just been a great big party when I look at my statements." Sure–let's talk about the sale of the Brooklyn Bridge.

REASON NUMBER 6: "I believe those no-advice," I mean–
"no-caring," oops,
"no-clue," sorry,
"no-help," Rats! I did it again didn't I?

I believe those **no-load** funds that sell to a mass market really do care about me as much as my politicians do. Yeah, that's the ticket.

REASON NUMBER 5: "Since CNBC is *never* wrong, I can go there to get all the financial advice I need."

Rrrright.

REASON NUMBER 4: "I get my advice from a highly reliable source."

My neighbor, my co-worker, my dart board . . .

REASON NUMBER 3: "I believe financial publications that depend on advertising revenue from no-this, no that, no way, no- load funds can render the impartial and objective advice I need."

Am I beating a dead horse here?

REASON NUMBER 2: "I would much rather deal with a 20-year-old clerk on the other end of an 800-number in some other part of the country than have access to an actual professional in my area."

Sending my hard-earned life savings through the mail to total strangers at no-help funds gives me peace of mind.

AND THE NUMBER ONE REASON WHY PEOPLE INVEST ON THEIR OWN: "I just don't know what else to do."

It's okay to admit you don't know what to do. It takes a lot of guts to do that. It's one thing to get into trouble, but it's often pride that keeps us there. Let me show you what you will be missing if you are strong enough to admit that you need guidance when it comes to investing:

People who invest on their own think that by investing in mutual funds, they will be okay. Let's look at some historical data. During the 1973–74 bear market, mutual funds took a big hit. Below is a chart that shows how many years it took for some of the more popular funds to get back to their pre-bear market levels.

1973-74 Bear Market

"I'm Well Diversified in Mutual Funds."

	Loss	**Back to 197:**
Fidelity Magellan Fund	-52%	1978
20 th Century Growth	-53%	1976
Nicholas Fund	-69%	1981
Templeton Growth	-46%	1976
Investment Co. of America	-45%	1978
AIM Weingarten	-65%	1978
Washington Mutual	-36%	1977
Vanguard Windsor	-47%	1978
IDS New Dimensions	-58%	1980
Janus Funds	-37%	1978

"Hey, no problem. I only deal in large cap companies."

1973-74 Bear Market

"I'm Well Diversified in Blue-Chip Stock."

	Loss	**Back to 197:**
Coca-Cola	-70%	1986
General Electric	-60%	1982
Pepsico	-67%	1979
Phillip Morris	-50%	1980
Walt Disney	-85%	1986
Electric Utility Index	-60%	1985
Merck	-53%	1985
Wal-Mart	-75%	1978
Exxon	-46%	1976
S&P Bond Index	-22%	1979

According to this information, if you purchased Walt Disney stock before 1973, it dropped 85% in value and took *twelve years* to make it back to even. (1974 to 1986).

Let me ask you a question; would you invest with my company if I could promise to:

- Lose 37% of your money once every 5 years
- Take 18 months for it to go down so much
- Take 36 months to make it back to even
- Offer a 10.5 average return if you stay in for 75 years
- Admit that there is a 99.984% chance you won't do this well

Would you invest with me? No? I can't imagine why not. What I've just described to you is the S & P 500. I hope I have made this point quite clear that it is in your best interest to seek a professional financial advisor when you are ready to take the retirement plunge. Don't step over dollars to save dimes. Yes, a good broker will cost you some money, but the money he can potentially make and save for you will be worth it.

HERE ARE SOME THINGS I WANT YOU TO AVOID WHEN IT COMES TIME TO SELECT AN INVESTMENT REPRESENTATIVE.

1. When seeking a professional to help manage your retirement dollars, consider the word "professional." Many of my colleges manage accounts for individuals from 0 to 99. Although this is not a reason for red flags, it would be to your advantage to find a broker that deals primarily with your stage in life. Retirement planning and implementing is extremely complex and equally important. Make sure your financial planner is qualified to handle your needs.

    In his autobiography, baseball great Nolan Ryan tells the secret of his longevity; hours and hours of workout. He spent five hours on the track or in the weight room or in some other form of strenuous endeavor. A lot of people were amazed to see him on an exercise bicycle immediately after a game while his arm was being iced.

Ryan's daily routine of exercising might sound boring to many of us. It might seem like he wasted time doing it. But he said it was necessary if he wanted to be at peak condition every time he stepped out on the diamond. Ryan wanted to be ready every time his number was called.

That is the kind of broker you are looking for; one that doesn't stop learning and growing. I read an article recently that said some doctor's are so busy they are about two years behind the medical discoveries. That's scary. I've asked you to keep growing throughout this book, can you expect any less from your broker?

2. Be sure you understand what "fee-base only" firms are. Simply put, fee based accounts are accounts that are charged an annual percentage of its value for services rendered. This means you will pay an annual management or maintenance fee even if there is a loss in the account value. There are many different philosophies on this subject and I don't want to sound like this type of pay structure is never appropriate. However, if you plan to buy and hold your retirement investments, a commission-based, AKA a transaction-based service would more than likely be appropriate. If, on the other hand, you plan to make multiple trades or you want your advisor to have the authority to make trades on your behalf, then a fee-based structure might be what you need. My advice is talk to both types of brokers and weigh the pros and cons together. It can save you money and aggravation along the way.

3. Watch out for churning. Churning is a term used in the investment world to describe excessive buying and selling of securities using the same money. If a broker has a reputation of making multiple trades using the same

money, it can be due to the fact that the trades are for generating commissions and not for the benefit of the client. For the most part, brokers trade when they feel it is necessary, but there is usually a bad apple or two in every basket.

4. Avoid a "hybrid" broker i.e. one who tries to do it all. This takes our first avoidance danger to the next level. Avoid an advisor that sells insurance, real estate, stocks, bonds, used cars, antiques, etc. etc. A sign read:

"Veterinarian and Taxidermist"
~ Either Way You Get Your Dog Back ~

Let me reiterate my caution expressed in my first point: find a true specialist who knows what you need and who won't try to sell you a life policy and a vintage pinto with low miles at the same time.

CONCLUSION:

Treat your quest for a financial advisor like an employer looking for the right employee to fill a specific position in your company. Prepare a list of questions to ask during the "interview" process. A question I am often asked is, "How do you make your money?" I think that is a fair question. Hard working people know that brokers have to make a living too, so if you get a vague answer or feel the response falls short, look for another broker to interview.

As I mentioned in point number two, a broker receives compensation in one of two ways. Either he is paid a *commission* for each transaction he executes or he receives a *fee* for managing an individual's portfolio. Each payment type has pros and cons, depending on the needs and goals of the investor. It is important to know which imbursement mode your potential financial consultant uses in order for you to make an educated decision when choosing an advisor.

Personally, I prefer to charge a transaction fee. It is simply a personal preference that I have used throughout my advisor career. I tell my clients what each transaction will cost and whether the fee is charged on the front end, or the back end. Most of the time there is no fee on either end if the client stays in the selected fund for a pre-determined period of time.

When asking questions, watch out for political answers; i.e. answers to the wrong question. If the broker does not answer the question you asked, keep looking.

An elderly lady entered a pet store hoping to purchase a parrot. The store manager did have a parrot, but he warned the little lady about purchasing this particular bird. For you see, this parrot had been raised by a sailor and had picked up much of the sailor's strong language. Confident she could rehabilitate the parrot, though, the elderly lady purchased it.

Upon arriving at its new home and being placed in a wonderful new cage, the parrot began an unbelievable barrage of shocking words. Immediately, the elderly lady removed the parrot from its cage and placed it in her freezer.

After five minutes she retrieved the parrot and replaced it in the cage. Solemnly she asked, "Now, what do you have to say?" Feathers shaking and beak rattling, the parrot began another shocking onslaught.

Determined, the little lady returned the parrot to the freezer once more, this time for ten minutes. Again she asked, "Now what do you have to say? Are you going to curse again?"

Though he was shivering mightily, the obstinate parrot let loose another torrent of foul (no pun intended) language. Back in the freezer he went, this time for fifteen minutes. He almost didn't survive. The little lady pulled him out just in the nick of time and asked him once more if he was going to continue to curse. Blue in color, feathers frozen stiff, and an icicle hanging

A Funny Thing Happened on My Way to Work . . . I Retired

from its beak the parrot replied, "N-n-n-no, m-m-maam! B-b-but could you please tell me what that t-t-t-turkey in there said?"

The moral of this story; it's not good to be a turkey if you're a broker. If you're not getting the response you want from the interview process, put the broker back in the freezer. Don't be uncomfortable asking questions. It's your money. Ask all the questions you can think of.

"The sun, which has all those planets revolving about it and depending on it for their orderly functions, can ripen a bunch of grapes as if it had nothing else in the world to do."

-Galileo

CHAPTER TEN

Returning to the Crow's Nest

Let's see. We've gotten our sea legs, built our ship, survived the tumultuous seas, avoided icebergs and torpedoes, found the SS Minnow and wisely chose our Captain. What is left for us to do?

Pick your island. (Boy, this is the best part). What do you want to do now?

Below are some thought provoking questions to ask yourself now that you have survived the strenuous data-gathering stage. Have some fun with this!

1. Where do you want to live?
2. Will you work part-time? Will you start your own business?
3. What hobbies/activities will you be involved in?
4. How will you spend your free time?
5. Will you be caring for an elderly or disabled person?
6. What goals were unachievable during the working years? Can they be reached now?
7. Will you volunteer at the library, church, or a children's hospital? (They can always use baby rockers).
8. Do you want to travel? Where to? Will you go RVing or get a touring motorcycle?
9. Will you go back to school?
10. Will you remodel the house or plant a garden?
11. Will you write a book? (It is a wonderful experience)

12. Will you get that boat in the water or those golf clubs out of the garage?
13. Will you spoil your grandkids? Need I ask this one?

I will leave these questions for you to ponder. What I want to address in this chapter is something that is probably low on your priority list or, more likely, it is under your radar altogether, yet it is one of the most important ingredients in a successful, happy retirement. Many people consider this a non-issue until the bottom falls out. What am I talking about? **Getting reacquainted with your spouse**.

Back on my farm in Indiana, we had a large patch of woods full of squirrels. On the south side of the woods was a natural lake. (It was more like a very large pond). To this day I have never seen, fished, or swam in that lake. Why? When I was a very young boy, our neighbor decided to irrigate his fields using the fresh water from the lake. He watered, and watered, and watered until he had used up most of the water in the lake. What happened next was a surprise to all.

The best anyone can figure is this; when the water was pumped out, it was drained too quickly causing a sudden loss of pressure. This, in turn, caused the soft bottom of the lake to rise, which consequently sucked in the surrounding dirt. Two things happened, both of them bad. First, the center of the lake was shallower now than the surrounding edges. Since Indiana gets a great deal of rain, it formed a quicksand barrier that completely encircled the water.

Second, sucking in the dirt caused the sub-terrain water to wash out deep crevasses several feet below the surface. My dad almost lost a tractor and his life by sinking into one of these "bottomless" pits in the field.

All of this occurred because a careless farmer changed the natural essence of a lake too quickly for it to adjust and now it is no more than a useless swamp.

Going from work to home will be a sudden change for

you and for your spouse, perhaps too sudden. If both of you are not prepared for this change the result can be disastrous. I am not just talking about the husband here. Most American families enjoy a dual income from both spouses. According to a Family Circle survey of 35,000 women, the time-crunch of work and family is hard on a marriage. 50% of the women say that there are never enough hours in a day, and another 33% say there are only sometimes enough hours. When asked what they have to put on the back burner to squeeze everything in, 51% said "friends" and 25% said "husbands." 75% of the women said that time factors were negatively effecting times of intimacy with their spouses. (In the June, 1989 issue of *Psychology Today,* "Time-poor women: housekeeping goes first." Pg 12).

Working people are desperate to squeeze just a few more minutes into every day.

A young wife called a newspaper office and asked for the food editor.

"Would you please help me?" She asked. "I'm cooking a special dinner tonight for my husband's boss and his wife. I've never cooked a big dinner before, and I want everything to be perfect. I bought a nine-pound turkey. Could you tell me how long to cook it in my new microwave?"

"Just a minute," the food editor said, as he turned to check his reference book.

"Oh, thank you," she said. "You've been a big help. Good-bye!"

Life is busy. We can all relate to the fact that there are not enough hours in the day and not enough days in the week.

Now, imagine spending years working this difficult schedule and then suddenly stopping. To be frank, you and your spouse are accustomed to, at least, one of you leaving the house to go to work five days a week. What happens when you or they don't leave anymore? I hear my clients joke about keeping the retiring spouse busy and out of the house. There is truth in jesting. Many couples are nervous about the forced closeness that's

A Funny Thing Happened on My Way to Work . . . I Retired

coming. Guess what? Those feelings are real and oftentimes valid. Don't dismiss them as just something to deal with when the time comes.

When I was a youth minister in Lumberton, Texas, I saw a couple's marriage fall apart because of this "syndrome." The kids were gone and they both retired. We had long talks about them getting to know each other again, but the strain was more than they could bear and they ended up getting a divorce.

Once a reporter asked the French diplomat, Robert Schuman, why he had never married. "Years ago, I was riding on the subway," Schuman replied. "Quite by accident, I stepped on the dainty foot of a pretty woman. As I turned to apologize, she barked, 'You clumsy idiot! Why can't you watch where you're going?' But when she looked up and saw me, she began to blush and said, 'Oh, so sorry sir. I thought you were my husband.'"

I hope your marriage is not like that *before* retirement. If it is, you have some work to do and the sooner you begin the better chance you'll have of avoiding an implosion. If you have a strong marriage, you may adjust well without much problem but why take the risk?

My wife and I have worked together most of our married life. For twelve years we ran a "mom and pop" business before I went back into the world of investments. She now works part-time as my computer operator and receptionist. Invariably, someone will ask us how in the world we can stand to work together? I tell them it is simple, as long as I say, "Yes ma'am and no ma'am, we get along just fine." I also tell them I hate it when she hollers, "Come out from under that bed and fight like a man!" I really hate that phrase.

Seriously, if someone cannot even dream of working with their spouse, how do they expect to spend time with them 24/7 and not go crazy? I've seen couples try to save their crumbling marriage by having a child, hoping that this would pull them back together. You already know the fallacy behind this thinking. Yet people tell themselves that taking the pressure of employment off the table will heal a wounded relationship. A prudent couple would do well to seek counseling PRIOR to any major change in their life. Take the opportunity during the calm season to prepare for the inevitable storm that is coming. Put this issue high on your 'to-do list' before retirement. Speaking of lists . . .

A couple was celebrating their 67th anniversary with friends. Someone asked the wife how she did it. "How did you stay married to the same man all these years?" The woman replied, "When we first got married, I made a secret vow that I would allow my husband to have ten bad habits that I would overlook. I was going to write these short comings on a piece of paper to remember them."

"What happened to the list?" a friend asked. Smiling, the woman said, "To tell the truth, I never got around to making the list. But, when my husband would do something that really annoyed me, I would say to myself, Lucky for him that one's on the list."

There are countless books out there on enriching your marriage. I've read many. Some are good and some aren't worth an amusement park token. What do you do? Let me offer a few suggestions that I believe will help prepare you for the "lake-draining" event that is coming.

1.   Start Dating. No not someone else, *each other*. I know you already go out to eat together and go to the movies but I am talking about REAL DATING. Plan a full and fun evening. Take time to be creative and romantic. Go parking after the movie. Hold hands when you walk together. Husbands, court your wives. Bring them flowers and candy. Wives plan an evening that focuses on your husband's desires. Don't say you're too old to do this. See my duck illustration in point number ten. One of my clients who is an 80 year old widower ran into his high school sweetheart a couple of weeks ago. She has been a widow for two years. They have started dating again and I've never seen him happier.

2. Take a Long Vacation Together Before Your Last Day of Work. This can be an excellent way to "test the waters" so to speak before you start spending extended time together. Get a feel for what it is going to be like. The key is "extended." Many times soon-to-be retirees have vacation days saved up. Don't just cash those in for money. Use them for something far more valuable. Use them as part of your "getting reacquainted" plan with your spouse. The longer the vacation the better. A quick note here. When making plans for this vacation, don't make the mistake of filling it up with too many activities. A vacation that is too busy can defeat the purpose of the exercise. By all means have fun, but make it fun in a way that involves the time and attention of both spouses.

3. Find a Retired Couple you Trust and get Advise. If nothing more, find some friends who will encourage you during your transition time. The Kisi people of Liberia, West Africa, have a proverb that goes like this: "When a man steps into the center of the circle to dance and no one claps, he will soon tire and sit down; but if everyone claps, he will dance all night." Find your cheering section. Look to your local church or community centers for inspiration. Use your hobbies as a starting point. I like to ride a motorcycle and my wife goes with me on group rides. We plan on taking some long trips together after the children are grown. If you can't find a group to belong to, MAKE ONE YOURSELF! I assure you there are other couples just like you who are looking for someone just like you. Find them!

Sometimes one word of encouragement may be all that stands between brilliant success and dismal failure. Here is a story a friend of mine told me that, I hope, will drive this point deep into your heart.

One day when I was a freshman in high school, I saw a kid from my class walking home from school. His name was Kyle. It looked like he was carrying all of his books. I thought to myself, "Why would anyone bring home all of his books on a Friday? He must really be a nerd."

I had quite a weekend planned—parties and a football game with my friends on Saturday afternoon—so I shrugged my shoulders and went on.

As I was walking, I saw a bunch of kids running towards him. They knocked all of his books out of his arms and tripped him so he landed in the dirt. His glasses went flying, and I saw them land in the grass about ten feet from him. As he looked up, I saw terrible sadness in his eyes. My heart went out to him. I jogged over to him as he crawled around looking for his glasses, and I saw a tear in his eye. As I handed him his glasses, I said, "Those guys are jerks. They should really get lives."

He looked at me and said, "Hey, thanks!" There was a big smile on his face. It was one of those smiles that showed real gratitude.

I helped him pick up his books and asked him where he lived. As it turned out, he lived near me, so I asked him why I hadn't seen him before. He said he had gone to private school before now.

We talked all the way home, and I carried some of his books. He turned out to be a pretty cool kid, and we hung out all weekend. The more I got to know Kyle, the more I liked him, and my friends all felt the same. Over the next four years, Kyle and I became best friends.

Since Kyle was the valedictorian of our class, he had to prepare a speech for graduation. I was so glad it wasn't me having to get up there and speak! Kyle was one of those guys who had really found himself during high school. He'd filled out and actually looked good in glasses. He'd also had more dates than I had, and all of the girls loved him.

I could tell he was nervous about the speech, so I

smacked him on the back and said, "Hey, big guy, you'll be great!" "Thanks," he replied. A few minutes later, he cleared his throat and began his speech.

"Graduation is a time to thank those who helped you make it through the tough years—your parents, your siblings, maybe a coach . . . but mostly your friends. I am here to tell you that being a friend to someone is the best gift you can give. I'd like to tell you a story."

I listened in disbelief as my best friend told the story of the day we met. He had planned to kill himself over that weekend. He spoke about how he had cleaned out his locker so his mom wouldn't have to do it later . . . that was why he was carrying so much stuff home.

Kyle added, "Thankfully, I was saved. My friend saved me from doing the unspeakable." I heard a gasp go through the crowd as this handsome, popular boy told us all about his weakest moment. I saw his mom and dad looking at me and smiling the same grateful smile Kyle often displayed. It was only then that I realized its depth.

Never underestimate the power of your actions. With one small gesture, you can truly change a person's life—for better or for worse.

4. **Find Common Interests and Build on Them.** You have been apart almost as much as you have been together. Like most, you tried to steal time together to do things as a family. Find those areas in your life that you both enjoy and build on them. If you both like to fish or play golf go for it. This *doesn't* mean that you must play golf together every time you hit the fairway, but there will be times when you will plan to play together.

I took a break from writing just now and walked across the parking lot to a new mom and pop store. I met the owners who are husband and wife. He retired from being a pharmacist two years ago and they began to travel. He said he felt like he was no longer contributing to society and wanted to get back into the work force. He and his wife decided to open a little store together. They seem very happy working with each other. They both like working in retail and both have extensive experience being self-employed. This is an excellent example of my earlier point.

Another couple that are good friends have decided to open their home to foster children. I had the privilege of writing a recommendation for them a few months ago. It is a long process, but they are so excited. This is something they can accomplish together. Find your common ground and start planting.

5.   Talk About your Pet Peeves with Each Other. George Carlin once quipped, "Have you ever noticed that when you're driving, everyone going slower than you is an 'idiot' and everyone going faster than you is a 'maniac'?"

You've got to tell your spouse what "speed" you like to go. This should not be delivered or received as nagging or accusations. It is designed to help each of you avoid unnecessary stress. Many times the offending spouse has no idea they are displaying irritable behavior and would be glad to change if they knew it bothered you. But you have to *tell* them. You also have to listen.

David Burns, a medical doctor and professor of psychiatry at the University of Pennsylvania, says: "The biggest mistake you can make in trying to talk convincingly is to put your highest priority on expressing *your ideas and feelings*. What most people really want is to be listened to, respected, and understood. The moment people see that they are being understood, they become more motivated to understand your point of view."

6.   If Necessary, Seek Professional Help. I mentioned this earlier and I can't say it enough, there is nothing wrong with going to a marriage counselor. When I was in Seminary at Southwestern Baptist Seminary, I discovered that there was a marriage counselor department on campus. This clinic was there to help seminary students deal with the struggle of going to school full time and working full time. If men and women who are studying for the ministry or mission field need a marriage counselor on campus, we should not consider it odd if we need one for retirement.

7. **Practice Communicating.** This goes along with suggestion number five. Learn to communicate with each other. Men and women think so differently it is easy to misunderstand what one is trying to say.

Do you remember the telegram messages that were a primary source of communication once upon a time? Did you ever wonder why the word "stop" was used at the end of each sentence? The following story just might be the reason for adopting this strange use of punctuation. At any rate, it makes a great point.

Once there was a wealthy man who ran his business in the United States and in England. On occasion his wife would travel across the channel to take care of business issues for her husband and enjoy a little shopping on the side. On one such occasion, she found a beautiful necklace in a jewelry store. The price for the rare find was $50,000. She knew her husband would not agree to such an exorbitant amount of money for a piece of jewelry, but she thought she would try anyway.

She sent a wire to the US and asked her husband if she could make the purchase. His reply was simple, "No. Price too high." Unfortunately, somewhere in the process the period didn't get printed so the wife received the message, "No Price too High." She bought the necklace. After an expensive lawsuit, the telegraph company began to use the word "stop" in place of a period.

I was watching an old classic war movie starring Jimmy Stewart. He was in the Air Force and was called away to service just prior to his daughter being born. After his wife had the baby, she sent a message to him asking what she should name their new bundle of joy. His reply was, "Can't think of any name but hope everything is fine. When he finally returned home he was met at the door by his wife and his new baby girl, who was named... you guessed it, Hope. She read the message as, "Can't think of any name but Hope. Everything is fine." Surprised?

Work on communication with your spouse. Make sure you understand each other. Be honest with each other even if it means hurting someone's feelings. I'm certainly not advocating that you intentionally say hurtful things to your spouse. What I am talking about here is something much, much deeper.

This next statement might be the most difficult thing I will ask you to do in this book but it is an appropriate request and it is imperative that I address it. The statement is this: If you have a dark secret that you have kept from your spouse for months or years, *find a way to tell him/her about it and if necessary, seek their forgiveness.* Sometimes it is easier to avoid feelings of guilt when you are not constantly confronted with its memory. As you spend more time together, the old skeletons in the closet will start finding their way out. They will surface as anger, depression, anxiety, drinking or they will make you physically ill. The *only* cure for this malady is to get it off your chest. If you feel that telling your spouse is too great a risk at this point, tell a trusted friend, or your pastor, but tell someone! It may break a heart but it can heal a marriage. Your marriage is stronger than you think.

In the classic Russian novel *Crime and Punishment,* a young student murders two people for their money. He rationalizes his crime by telling himself, first, that Napoleon killed thousands and became a hero; second, that his victims were unimportant people; and third, that he would use the money to further his career for the good of humanity. Most of the story, however, is taken up not with the crime but with the young student's punishment—punishment not from without but from within. Guilt rages inside, and his body, mind and spirit grind away at each other and wear him down.

There is a young girl in the novel, Sonia, who loves this young murderer. Hers is a rare kind of love. It is not cheap sentiment. First of all, her love drives him to confess that he is the murderer. She tells him he must do penance to try and expiate his guilt. He does. He kisses the ground he had stained with human blood and cries out his confession to the four corners of the earth. Finally, he is convicted and sent off to Siberia, suffering from tuberculosis and pneumonia. But the story doesn't end there. The girl, Sonia, follows him over the hard miles to Siberia. Throughout his long nine-year sentence, she stays by his side. She keeps them both alive by scrounging whatever food she can find. Her love for him never gives up.

Take the risk and tell him/her. Psychologists have used the term "scruples" to describe the person whose sense of guilt over past deeds tends to restrict future accomplishments. The word "scruple" is derived from the Latin word, *scrupulum*. A scrupulum is a small pebble. When by accident a small pebble gets lodged inside one of our shoes, we feel intermittent stabs of pain as we walk. So, the scrupulous person, as he walks through life, feels the intermittent agonies of guilt. End it today.

8.   Just Say No. Now that you have absolutely "nothing" to do, which is what most people think about newly retired individuals, you will be asked to volunteer for everything from rocking babies to being a foster parent for unwanted porcupines. Don't fall into the trap of replacing one busy lifestyle for another. I said staying home was an adjustment, I didn't say it will always be a bad one. Your spouse may be counting the days until you can wake up in the morning and stay home. It is important that you remain active after retirement, but stay active for the right reasons. Don't use busyness as an excuse to spend less time in the house. If you want to volunteer, go for it, but not because you are afraid the walls will close in on you or, more importantly, because you aren't comfortable with saying, 'no.'

9.   Plan to Keep Some Activities Separate. You don't have to do everything together now that you are retired.

Certainly make time for each other but don't become something you're not. We are complex, multifaceted beings in need of diverse relationships. No one person is designed to meet all of the needs of another. Men need male companionship and women need female companionship. Let me address one other point here. If you have grown children, or children that are close to college age, they need you now more than ever. What better way to help guide them through their tumultuous years than by taking a son fishing or a daughter for a long woman-to-woman drive in the country.

10. Finally, Don't Stop Growing Together.

He was one of the greatest soldiers of his time. He lived at a time when his country needed great soldiers! Yet his past so discouraged him that he almost never became the leader that his country needed.

Hiram was born to a father who was harsh and cold and would always see him as a failure. His mother was not a source of emotional comfort to him either; he never once saw her moved enough to shed a tear. Hiram was always small for his age. He grew up ashamed he was not the kind of leader his father expected him to be.

At age 17, his father pressured him into joining the U. S. Military Academy. Hiram was now 5' 1" and 120 pounds. He feared failing. He hated the school, but he dared not buck his father's decision. In fact, when the academy listed his name wrong, the young man was too timid even to get the error corrected. He went through the rest of his life under a partly erroneous name.

In time, Hiram settled into the school and did acceptably—graduating just below the middle of his class. When he returned home, though, his neighbors mocked him in his new uniform, and the old humiliation returned. The boy was so deeply wounded emotionally that he would forever feel self-conscious in uniform. Later, as a 3-star general, he would prefer to wear a simple private's shirt with 3 stars sewn on it.

A Funny Thing Happened on My Way to Work . . . I Retired

After marrying and attaining the rank of Captain, he dropped out of the military. He tried various ventures in civilian life until the Civil War broke out. He then tried to re-enlist as an officer. He found it hard even to get an interview with someone who could appoint him to a position.

Only a few good strokes of fortune ever made it possible for Hiram to show what kind of a military leader he really was. But he truly was a leader! For the young man who lived with a sense of inadequacy, who never had any great physical stature, and who almost couldn't make it in a career was named Hiram Ulysses Grant. We remember him as Ulysses S.; Grant, leader of the victorious Northern Army and later President of the United States. (Mark Grimsley. "Ulysses S. Grant" His Life and Hard Times," *Civil War Times Illus.* (Feb., 1990), pp. 21–25.

Yogi Berra was right, "It ain't over till its over."

You haven't reached the pinnacle in your marriage or your life. If you have time before retirement take dance lessons together or enroll in a photography class. Find something that neither one of you knows how to do and learn together. It can be a load of fun. If you stop growing together, you run the risk of growing apart.

Soren Kierkegaard once told a story about a wild duck flying south with other ducks. Below him in a barnyard he noticed some corn a farmer had scattered for his tame ducks. So the duck broke formation and joined the tame ducks in the barnyard. He ate the corn, liked it, and decided to stay a few days.

The corn was free and life was easy, so he stayed longer. Spring eventually came. And one day, high overhead, the duck heard his wild mates calling as they flew by on their way back north. Their call reminded him of his true life, but when he tried to rejoin them, he could no longer fly. He had settled for ease and comfort. He had given in to a life of collecting corn off of the ground. He became a commodity for the farmer's table.

We must keep growing if we are going to keep flying. Age is totally irrelevant when it comes to growing as a person and as a spouse. Since birds of a feather flock together, we as couples would do well to do the same.

CONCLUSION:

We have covered a great deal of information in this chapter. Soul searching can be very tiring and often times painful. Some of these areas I have addressed may have struck a nerve that has been buried deep in your psyche. If that is the case and you don't know what to do, or you would like to talk to someone who cares and who is not qualified to throw the first stone, I would encourage you to seek out a pastor in your area. As a former pastor and an investment consultant, I have seen the best and the worst in people but I have *never* seen a person or marriage that was not worth saving. Also, I have seen ministers of various denominations and experience reach out and help families climb out of an otherwise devastating situation. If you have a need that goes beyond the scope of this book, find a local pastor and you might find the answers you seek.

"Keep doing what you're doing and you'll get what you've got"

-Anonymous

CHAPTER ELEVEN

CAPTAIN'S LOG

Captain Kirk had the right idea when he entered important events into the 'Captain's Log.' I forget the star date but it was impressive. (I remember when the episodes were run for the first time. You do too, don't you?).

As the time is winding down to the "Big Day," there is one more housekeeping item we need to consider:

ORGANIZING ALL OF YOUR PAPERWORK.

This serves a four-fold purpose:

Having your paperwork organized will come in handy when you make the trip to the Social Security office.

It will help you be more accurate when you sit down to do your tax returns and it can help you avoid having to pay a CPA to recreate your records.

You will do your loved ones a *huge* favor when the time comes for you to sail into the great beyond. There seems to be no end to the sad tales I've heard about heirs who were left with utter chaos because their deceased loved one didn't take the time to get their "house in order."

When all the documents are gathered, you can put them together in a safe place. It would not be a bad idea to make copies of valuable documents and keep them in a different facility.

So, like every other exercises in this book, don't cut this one short. You may think you have everything in order, but look again. You may be surprised.

A Funny Thing Happened on My Way to Work . . . I Retired

IMPORTANT DOCUMENTS   Check if Current

Social Security cards ❏
Birth Certificates ❏
Marriage Certificates ❏
    Prenuptial Agreements ❏
    Divorce Papers ❏
    Child Custody Papers ❏
Adoption Papers ❏
Death Certificates ❏
Naturalization Papers ❏
Residency Papers ❏
Military Papers ❏
Wills ❏
Deeds (Don't forget cemetery plots) ❏
Old Tax Returns: Five years is best ❏
Insurance ❏
    Health ❏
    Home/Property ❏
    Auto ❏
    Life ❏
    Disability ❏
Mortgage Papers ❏
Contracts ❏
Auto Registration and Title ❏
Bank Books ❏
Check Books ❏
Stock and Bond Certificates ❏
Credit Card Statements ❏
Other Records: ❏
    _____ ❏
    _____ ❏
    _____ ❏
    _____ ❏

Some of these categories may seem unrelated to retirement, but they are all part of the planning process, excluding, of course, the ones that do not apply. The harder you work to get your papers in order, the more carefree your retirement can be.

TRANSFERING WEALTH

Robert Raines tells a beautiful story about a young man named David who left home for the first time. From the age of seven he had lived with his uncle and aunt, who sold fruit at a peddler's stand. They had loved and cared for him. He stood on the train platform getting ready to leave. He grabbed the rough hands of his peddler-uncle and said, "How can I ever begin to repay you for what you've done for me!"

His uncle spoke: "David, there's a saying, 'The love of parents goes to their children, but the love of these children goes to their children.'"

"But," David protested: "That's not so. I'll always be trying to . . ."

And then the aunt interrupted, "David, what your Uncle Asher means is that a parent's love isn't to be paid back; it can only be passed on." (Robert Raines, Creative Brooding, New York: Macmillan, 1966, pp. 102–103

You probably think I'm a little presumptuous talking about transferring wealth at the dawn of your retirement, but, as I tell my kids, "It's better to have it and not need it, than to need it and not have it." Our kids are worth it.

There is a Kenyan proverb that goes like this: "Treat the Earth well. It was not given to you by your parents, it was loaned to you by your children."

A revocable living trust is a powerful instrument, which can make the transfer of wealth from one generation to the next, a simplified process. Allow me to spend a little time explaining the difference between a living trust and a will. It is vital that we know the difference between these two words. Simple misunderstanding of a single word can have dire consequences.

I have heard that during the closing weeks of World War II, the Allies issued the Potsdam Ultimatum to Japan. The emperor of Japan wished to end the war in July, 1945. The Japanese announced a policy of "MOKUSATSU" which can mean to ignore completely; or to simply refrain from comment. The Japanese wished to refrain from comment until they could weigh fully the terms of the ultimatum.

Unfortunately, a press dispatch translated the word, "Mokusatsu" to mean that the cabinet would ignore the ultimatum. The erroneous interpretation was allowed to stand. The war was prolonged. Atomic bombs fell on Nagasaki and Hiroshima. Thousands perished, others were horribly maimed for life, all because one word was misinterpreted. Obviously we are not talking about mass destruction and loss of life, but we *are* talking about the difference between the transfer of wealth in peace verses a pending war over what you leave behind. Make sure you understand the difference between a will and a living trust. Let's begin with the will.

A WILL

Many people believe that if they have a will, they will avoid probate. ***This is wrong!*** Having a will is an engraved invitation to the probate party. For a will to have any legal effect, it *must* be submitted for probate.

Probate can be time consuming and frustrating. On average, probate takes somewhere between six months and two years or longer. If you want your family to have immediate access to your property upon your death, you don't want probate. If you own property in other states, probate will have to be opened in *every* state where the property is located. Some heirs have simply abandoned property in other states because the cost of probate exceeded the value of the property itself.

What if you are disabled? If you become mentally disabled, your property is "frozen" until the probate court appoints a conservator to manage your financial affairs. Example: You are disabled; your home and your investments generally cannot be sold, EVEN IF OWNED IN JOINT TENANCY, until a conservator is appointed. This usually involves filing fees, attorney's fees, accounting fees, and court orders, all designed to "protect" the disabled person.

You can minimize estate taxes with a will but all too often beneficiaries continue to hold their property in joint tenancy, which may allow them to avoid probate, however, they also avoid the tax savings created by the will. This can be a devastating error in titling property.

Probate is a matter of public record. It is a legal process initiated and paid for by your family. In some cases, salesmen will gain a copy of the will to add to their prospecting list. It is perfectly legal for them to do this.

Wills are easy to contest; a simple letter to the judge can tie up assets for months or even years.

I know at this point it sounds like I am dead set against having a will. Not necessarily. I just want you to be aware of the downside to owning a will. There can, however, be an upside. There are times when a will is appropriate. Young couples who possess the following qualities may find a will appropriate. Couples who:

1. Are in good health
2. Own no out-of-state property
3. Have small estates
4. Are likely to have family changes like marriage, divorce or children
5. Are less concerned about probate and publicity.

In a situation similar to this, a will is usually more cost

efficient. However, the day may come, and probably will, when they will need to move from a will to a trust. I did.

A TRUST

There are many kinds of trusts. I am referring to a fully funded *Revocable Living Trust,* under which you would serve as the Trustee. You would then proceed to transfer all of your assets into the trust. Because you are the trustee, you keep total control of your assets.

Having a trust will not complicate your tax return as some fear. You will file just as you have always done in the past on form 1040. To use an analogy, think of the trust as a person that can't die. While you are alive, you can do what you want to with your property without the supervision of the courts. If you transfer all of your assets to your trust, it, in essence, becomes the owner of the assets. You still control every aspect of the property, but when you die, the living trust can disperse the property just as if you were doing it yourself, hence, no probate, and no contesting, resulting in no delays for heirs.

Trusts remain private and are not subject to the publicity that a will is. No salesmen can add you to their prospect list. Since it is a private matter, there is no need to send notice to disinherited heirs; no inventory, not even a copy of your trust is required to be filed. As a rule, trusts are far more difficult to be challenged.

There are disadvantages to setting up a trust. One such disadvantage is the cost to create one. A trust generally costs more than a will ($300 for a will verses $600~$1,500 or more for the trust). Be sure to shop around for price and quality. Ask friends who have a trust who they used and if they would recommend them to you. Ask a potential trust attorney to show you a sample trust. Ask what other documents are included. Find out what assistance they will provide in transferring your assets into the trust. You will want an experienced trust provider who believes in trust planning. One other source is your financial advisor. Technically they are unable to offer legal or tax advice, but they generally have a great deal of knowledge about trusts due to the fact that some of their clients will have accounts opened up in the name of a trust. I have many such accounts and I work closely with a trust attorney on behalf of my clients.

Below is a simple list to help you determine which avenue you wish to pursue.

FACTORS TO CONSIDER	USE A WILL	USE A TRUST
Age	Young/Under 40	Older/Over 55
Concern about incapacity Or probate	Good Health	Poor Health
Family situation	Simple	Complex
Desire for privacy	Low	High
Size of Estate	Small	Taxable or nearly so
Out-of-state property	None	Any
Current status	Up-to-Date Will	Simple Will or none
Desire to protect family	None needed	Strong Desire
Likelihood of Contest	Little or none	Some chance

In case you haven't noticed by now, my assumption here is that you will establish either a will or a trust. Don't even consider not having either! I have illustrated a "none will" below that I hope will give you some idea about the perils of not having a will or living trust.

LAST WILL AND TESTAMENT OF MR I. B. WAITEN (Who Died *Without* A Will)

I Mr. I. B. Waiten of Procrastinate, Arkansas do hereby make, publish and declare this to be my Last Will and Testament.

FIRST ARTICLE

A. I give to my spouse, if she survives me, all of our community property and one-third of my separate property and give my two minor children the remaining two-thirds of my separate property.

B. I appoint my spouse as guardian of my children; but as a safeguard I require that she report to the County Probate Court each year and render an accounting of how, why and where she spent the money necessary for the proper care of our children. The children's estates shall pay all accountant and attorney fees to comply with this requirement.

C. As a further safeguard, I direct that my spouse pay for a surety bond to guarantee that she exercises proper judgment in the handling, investing and spending of our children's money.

D. Just in case, as a final safeguard, our children shall have the right to demand and receive, a complete accounting from their surviving parent of all her financial actions as soon as they reach legal age.

E. When our children reach eighteen, they shall have full rights to withdraw and spend their share of my estate. No one shall have any legal right to question their actions on how they decide to spend, or waste, their respective shares.

SECOND ARTICLE

A. If my spouse shall remarry, her second spouse may

receive everything my spouse possesses, if she should predecease him without executing a Last Will and Testament.
B. Should my still minor children need monies for their support; the second spouse is under no legal bounds to support them nor is he obligated to leave them anything in his Last Will and Testament.
C. The Second spouse may totally disinherit our children even after they are of legal age and everything my spouse brought into the second marriage from our marriage may go to his children alone to the exclusion of our children. Not sounding good so far? There's more.

THIRD ARTICLE

A. Should my spouse predecease me or die while any of our children are minors; I do not wish to exercise my rights as a parent to nominate the guardians of my minor children.
B. Rather, I direct that any and all of my relatives assemble together and fight over custody of my children in the County Probate Court.
C. In the event a consensus cannot be determined over who will be the guardians of my minor children; I direct that the County Probate Court make that decision even to the exclusion of any blood relative and the appointment of a complete stranger acceptable to it.

FOURTH ARTICLE

Under existing Arkansas tax law, there are certain legitimate avenues open to me to lower death taxes; however, since the State of Arkansas is currently drowning in red ink, I prefer to have my money used for probate fees, court costs, attorney's fees, filing fees, accounting costs, appraisal fees, arbitration costs, and other governmental purposes rather than avoiding these fees and passing more money to my heirs; I direct that no effort be made to lower taxes, avoid fees, and preserve more money for my family after my death.

FIFTH ARITICLE

I fully realize that this Last Will and Testament was written for me by an attorney and does not reflect my wishes or desires. I am truly sorry to my spouse and children that I did not have a Last Will and Testament, living trust, audio recording, handwritten note, or videotape of my final requests. I know that my indecision and lack of action has made my death a greater tragedy than it already is.

Perhaps this is a little over-simplified but it vividly conveys my point. Please don't be like the I. B's of the world. If you don't know where to begin, contact an estate or trust attorney. Many banks have a trust department that can steer you in the right direction.

"If you keep on saying that things are going to be bad, you have a good chance of being a prophet."

-Isaac Singer

CHAPTER TWELVE

DOCKING OUR SHIP

John Goddard, author of *Kayaks Down the Nile,* has been called a modern "Indiana Jones." He has climbed the highest mountains and has swum the deepest seas. He says that some of us wait so long for our ship to come in that our pier collapses. I am confident that if you have finished this book in its entirety, your ship will be docking soon and intact.

I hope I have made it clear in this book that life is about setting goals and working to reach them. It's like the man who was walking out in a huge meadow when he came across a bear that had lost her cubs. She gave him a glare then proceeded to rush towards him. Instinctively, he ran as fast as he could toward the nearest tree. It turned out this was the only tree in view and the nearest limb was at least fifteen feet off the ground. He could hear the bear gaining on him so he set a goal. "I have one chance," he told himself, "I have to reach that limb on the first jump." With all his might and just before the bear lunged at him he jumped for the limb. Unfortunately he missed it by about three feet . . . but he caught it on the way down. Man, that is goal setting!

How important is goal setting? There is a famous study involving graduates of Yale University of the class of 1953. It involves goal setting. Do you know where you are headed in life? Do you know how you are going to get there?

The graduates involved in these studies were asked if they had a clear, specific set of goals for their future. Were these goals written down with a plan for achieving them? It turned out that only 3 percent of those interviewed had such written goals.

A Funny Thing Happened on My Way to Work . . . I Retired

Twenty years later, in 1973, the researchers went back and interviewed the surviving members of the 1953 graduating class. They discovered that the 3 percent with written specific goals had achieved more in financial terms than the entire other 97 percent put together. They also seemed to be happier and more "together" in every way.

If you haven't done so, begin now to put your goals for retirement into writing. You have accomplished a great deal by working through each and every exercise and by gathering the documents I have assigned for you . . . **you did didn't you?**

"What is your number one goal for retirement?" This is a question I have asked many retirees and soon-to-be retirees. Invariably, I get the same response: "I want to have the freedom to make my own choices."

Isn't that what it's all about? Having the freedom to make your own choices? We talked in a previous chapter about money not being able to buy happiness. As true as that statement is, allow me to expound on it by adding a line to finish the thought. "Money can't buy happiness, but it can buy choices." Money alone is not going to bring purpose and meaning to your life or to the lives of your loved ones. However, it can be a tool and a means to a fulfilling life through choices. I didn't mention this earlier because I wanted to help you get your priorities lined up in the right order. Surveys say the number one reason couples argue is due to financial trouble. I didn't (and don't) want this to get in the way of your progress. If we spend all of our energy and time on the subject of money we will find ourselves bogged down and incapable of attending to other necessities in life.

In a book by Norman Vincent Peale, there is an account about a young man in North Carolina named Samuel A. Mann. Sam was tramping through the countryside. Being somewhat in a hurry he decided to go through a swamp rather than make a wide detour. He had on high hip boots and was slogging through the wet ground when he came to what looked like an area of dry sand. As he tried to cross it, he suddenly sank down to his knees.

As he tried to get back on solid ground, he realized a powerful suction gripped his legs like a vise, dragging him down deeper.

In a moment of complete horror he realized he was in a great pocket of quicksand. He remembered what the natives always said; "Nobody ever gets out of those quicksands alive."

For a moment he was paralyzed by panic, sinking deeper and deeper. To his left he saw some marsh grass growing, each blade perhaps half an inch wide. He thought to himself, "If I could just reach that grass, perhaps a handful would have the strength of a rope." He reached out his hand, but there was a gap of about three feet between his fingers and the marsh grass. He knew that if he lunged for the grass and missed it, he would disappear under the treacherous sand. If he did nothing, though, he was doomed.

By now, the sand was almost over the top of his hip boots. Suddenly he realized it wasn't the sand that was holding him. Rather the sand was holding his boots, which in turn were holding him. With shaking fingers he undid the straps that were holding his boots to his belt. Then, taking a deep breath and asking God to help him, he did it. He flung himself full length out of his boots across the deadly sand. His fingers touched the marsh grass. Desperately he grasped several strands. Then slowly, carefully, inch by agonizing inch; he pulled himself out of his boots onto the solid earth.

This story vividly illustrates the power of money. If our affection for it is too strong, it can slowly drag us down, smothering us, but, if we keep it in its proper perspective, it becomes a commanding ally. Unfortunately, many people allow money to be their obsession and, as a result, allow it to suck them down and squeeze the very joy of life out of them. One of the most miss-quoted verses in the Bible is: "Money is the root of all evil." The verse actually says: "The *love* of money is the root of all evil." Money is not evil, but our uncontrolled passion for it is. (Okay, enough preaching).

Let me close this chapter and book with a couple of case studies.

CASE STUDY I

I have a friend, Bill Luce, who recently retired from his job with the State of Arkansas. (Of course he went through the transition process with me.) He and his wife Sue dreamed of moving from their crowded suburban setting to a quiet home on the lake. Through careful planning and saving, and by following a well-designed exit plan from work into retirement, I am proud to report that their dream has come true. I ran into him the other day and asked how his retirement was going? His answer was predictable yet profound. He said that life had never been better. I know what you're thinking. "Well, of course he's happy. He's retired!" Or maybe your thought is: "He probably retired with a bunch of money." Well guess what? You gave one right answer but it's not the obvious one. He's not enjoying retirement just because he is retired, (I addressed this issue earlier in the book), but because he has earned the right to make *choices*. Approaching retirement without a clear-cut goal is like a blind man in a dark room searching for a black cat that isn't there. The end results will leave us disappointed and with very few options.

"Hey, I thought you said I was half right?" And you are. He did retire with a "bunch" of money. "Millions?" No. "Half a million?" Much less. "You said it was a bunch of money." It is . . . to him. That is the key I want you to burn into your inner brain. His lifestyle improved after retirement; making him a wealthy man. The dollar figures are unimportant when the goal of an improved quality of life has been reached.

CASE STUDY II

Let me tell you about another friend of mine who recently retired from Entergy. (You know what's coming don't you?) To be fair, he wasn't given much of a choice as to when he could retire due to policy changes in Entergy's insurance coverage. After we calculated his then current standard of living against his future standard, we discovered that he would have to forego some amenities, which he had grown accustomed to, in order to make ends meet. The only other option was for him to go back to work, which he did. He accepted a low paying position at a local Home Depot, selling electrical supplies.

But there is a bright spot to this story. Since he took the time to follow the right strategy in the retirement process, his rollover money is growing at a good pace. He will be able to leave his salesman job about the same time he would have retired from Entergy, and enjoy a standard of living he is used to.

Let me interject a note here. Not all stories have a happy ending like these two. The assumption in this book is that the upcoming retiree has utilized a disciplined savings plan during his working years. My goal of this book has been to pick up the story from there and bring it home. Planning to build a retirement nest egg is an entirely different book. Hmmm.

I trust that by now you know that simply retiring from your job will not bring unbounded joy and sunshine into your life forever and ever. To think it will be this way is as likely as throwing a calculator out in a field and coming back years later to find a NASA guidance computer has evolved from it. Life just doesn't work that way. The transition process must be handled correctly or the "golden" years will actually turn out to be the "pyrite" years.

As I mentioned in the first chapter, some people will experience as many years in retirement, if not more, than the time they spent in the workforce.

Let's revisit the story of the Titanic one more time. Confidence in the structure and stability of that massive floating palace was so high that the White Star Line was inclined to forego adding lifeboats. Fortunately for the 706 survivors, British law required lifeboats for vessels weighing over 10,000 tons. Twenty

A Funny Thing Happened on My Way to Work . . . I Retired

lifeboats were added reluctantly which, if loaded to capacity, could only hold less than have of the 885-crew members and 1,343 passengers on board the ship that fateful night.

When putting a retirement plan together, it is imperative to work "lifeboats" into the mix to guard against unplanned emergencies such as disability, long-term illness, or premature death. If you have made up your mind to follow the guidelines I have set forth in the preceding chapters, you have attached lifeboats to your retirement ship. As you know by now it doesn't matter how big your nest egg is, it can still be sunk.

For her maiden voyage, the mammoth ship carried enough food to feed a small town for several months. There was over sixty tons of fresh meat, fish, and poultry; forty tons of potatoes; 40,000 eggs; 7,000 heads of lettuce; over 100,000 pieces of fresh fruit, not including the 1,000 pounds of grapes. There were 3,000 pounds of coffee and tea and almost a ton of ice cream. There were 15,000 bottles of ales and stouts, 1,000 bottles of wine, and 8,000 cigars. She was a ship ready to meet the needs and desires of her passengers bountifully . . . then came the iceberg.

IN SUMMARY

You just succeeded in crossing the finish line . . . to the first race! Yes, there will be many other challenges crouching along your path waiting to pounce on you. But, the good news is you should now possess the basics necessary to deal with those challenges, and implement a satisfying retirement.

I am not so naïve as to believe that you have worked out every exercise, changed every attitude, and executed every task that I have set forth in this book. I also know some of the work seems tedious at best.

A little boy was playing in the front yard when he heard his mother call. He knew what she was going to ask him to do and he dreaded it. "Son, it's time to take this tray up to your grandfather's room and feed him lunch," said his mother. "Mom!" sighed the boy, "I hate feeding granddad. It's always so messy and kinda gross. Can't somebody else do it for a change?"

Seeing the resentment in her son's eyes, she stopped washing the dishes and sat down. "Let me tell you a story," she began. "Years ago, when you were just a baby, your grandfather was over for a visit. A fire suddenly broke out in the house. Your father and I met outside. I thought you were downstairs with your dad and he thought you were upstairs with me. When your grandfather saw what had happened, he immediately ran back into the burning house, found you, wrapped a blanket around you and managed to bring you out to safety. You were okay but your grandfather was severely burned. That is why he needs your help to eat everyday."

The little boy stood there with his mouth open. He couldn't believe is granddad had given up so much for him. Slowly, he turned and carefully carried the tray up to his granddad's room and began to feed him lunch. But something was different. This time the boy fed his grandfather, with a smile.

You didn't get to this place in life on your own. Someone, somewhere made sacrifices in order for you to succeed. If you don't make critical changes for yourself, do it for those around you.

Finally, if you need more answers to life than what I have provided in this book, let me suggest you read a best seller . . . the Bible.

HELPFUL WEBSITES AND DEFINITIONS:

WEBSITES

WWW.AARP.ORG This is a great site for retirees and soon-to-be retirees. It can provide help with health, finances and a host of other concerns.

WWW.SSA.GOV You can apply for social security or estimate your future check. This site provides answers to multiple questions raised by the retiree. You can go to the site for Medicare from this site.

WWW.PROFESSORBEYER.COM What happens to the dog or cat? Prof. Gerry Beyer of St. Mary's University School of Law in San Antonio provides an expert overview of estate planning that includes care for pets.

WWW.ELDERHOSTEL.ORG Fifty-fives and up can mix travel and learning through this venerable group. A few trips: exploring the culture of French Polynesia; a weekend in Richmond, Va.; a walk in Switzerland that welcomes grandkids 8 to 11.

WWW.BENEFITSCHECKUP.ORG This interactive site helps eligible elders find programs to assist with finances, housing, and other needs.

WWW.HEALTHFINDER.GOV Links to health information from government and other sources. Among the subjects: air pollution, hearing loss, and medical quackery. You can search for a doctor or details on a specific ailment.

WWW.BANKRATE.COM Calculators help you run the

numbers before deciding to refinance a mortgage, set up a savings plan, or move to a new city with a different cost of living.

WWW.VOLUNTEERMATCH.ORG Put spare time to good use with a database of local projects needing help. Among recent efforts: driving kids to camp and assisting with home fix ups.

WWW.GRANDSPLACE.COM Nearly 2.4 million grandparents are raising grandchildren. This support site includes guidance on legal rights and government aid.

DEFINITIONS:

A

ACCRUAL BONDS-Bonds that do not make periodic interest payments, but instead accrue interest until the bond matures. Also known as *zero-coupon bonds*.

ACCRUED INTEREST-Interest that has accumulated between the most recent payment and the sale of a bond or other fixed-income security.

ACQUISITION-One company taking over controlling interest in another company. Acquiring companies are sometimes willing to pay more than the market price for the shares they need to complete the acquisition.

ACTIVE MARKET-Heavy volume of trading in a particular security.

ANNUITY-Form of contract sold by life insurance companies that guarantees a fixed or variable payment to the annuitant at some future time, usually retirement.

ASKED PRICE-Generally it is the lowest round lot price at which a dealer will sell a security. (Wholesale)

B

BEAR MARKET-Prolonged period of falling prices.

BID-Highest price a prospective buyer is ready to pay. (Retail)

BIG BOARD-Popular term for the *NEW YORK STOCK EXCHANGE*

BLACK MONDAY-October 24, 1987, when the Dow Jones Industrial Average plunged a record 508 points.

BLUE CHIP-Common stock of a nationally known company that has a long record of profit, growth, and dividend payment and a reputation for quality management, products, and services. Examples: GE, Wal-Mart, IBM

BOLIER ROOM-Place where high-pressure salespeople use telephones to call lists of potential investors (known in the trade as A sucker list). *Watch out for this.*

BOND-Any interest-bearing security that obligates the issuer to pay the bondholder a specified sum of money, and to repay the principal amount of the loan at maturity.

BOND RATING-Method of evaluating the possibility of default by a bond issuer. The ratings range from AAA (highly unlikely to default) to D (already in default). Bonds rated below BBB- are not considered investment grade. (Example: BB rating is below investment grade).

BOOK-ENTRY-Securities are not in certificate form. It makes buying and selling the security easier. It also cuts down on paperwork and frees the investor from worrying about their certificates.

BULL MARKET-Prolonged rise in the prices of stocks or bonds. Bull markets usually last a few months or longer and are characterized by high trading volume.

BUY AND HOLD STRATEGY-Strategy that calls for accumulating shares in a company over the years. If held for more than a year and a day, it allows the investor to pay favorable long-term capital gains.

C

CALLABLE-Gives the issuer the right to buy back the bonds before the scheduled maturity date.

CHURNING-Excessive trading of a client's account for the purpose of generating commissions for the broker.

COMMON STOCK -Units of ownership (shares) of a public corporation.

CONSTANT DOLLAR PLAN (also known as Dollar Cost Averaging) Method of accumulating assets by investing a fixed amount of dollars in securities at set intervals. (Example: Buy $2000 worth of XYZ stock on the 5th of each month). The investor buys more shares when the price is low and fewer shares when the price is high.

COST BASIS-The original price of an asset, used in determining capital gains. It includes the market value of the stock when it was purchased and any commissions paid to make the purchase.

CURRENT YIELD-Annual interest on a bond divided by the market price. It is the actual income rate of return as opposed to the coupon rate (the two would be equal if the bond were bought at par) or the yield to maturity. The higher the market price of the bond, the lower the current yield will be. The opposite is also true. (Example: A bond paying 7% interest and costing $1050 would have a current yield of 6.67%. 7 divided by 1050 = .006666)

CUSTODIAL ACCOUNT-Account that is created for a minor. Minors cannot make securities transactions without the approval of the custodian who manages under the UNIFORM GIFTS TO MINORS ACT or the UNIFORM TRANSFERS TO MINORS ACT.

D

DATE OF RECORD-Date on which a shareholder must officially own shares in order to be entitled to a dividend.

DECLARATION DATE-Date on which a company

announces the amount and date of its next dividend payment. The investor must own the stock on the Date of Record in order to qualify for the dividend.

DEFINDED BENEFIT PLAN -Plan that promises to pay a specified amount to each person who retires after a set number of years of service. Some Defined Benefit Plans include a lifelong pension for the retired worker.

DEFINDED CONTRIBUTION PLAN-Includes 401(k), 403(b), and 457 plans. Unlike a Defined Benefit Plan, a Defined Contribution Plan can be taken as a lump sum or rolled into another tax-deferred vehicle such as an IRA.

DEFLATION-Decline in the prices of goods and services. Opposite of inflation.

DEPRESSED MARKET-Market characterized by more supply than demand and therefore weak (depressed) prices. (See DEFLATION).

DISCRETIONARY ACCOUNT-Account empowering a broker or advisor to buy and sell without the client's prior knowledge or consent. (Be careful with this).

DIVERSIFICATION-Spreading of risk by putting assets in several categories of investments-stocks, bonds, money market, or, spreading funds over different sectors of the economy-Health Sector, Consumer Sector, Energy Sector, etc.

DIVIDEND-Distribution of earnings to shareholders, prorated by class of security and usually paid in the form of money or stock. (See DATE OF RECORD).

E

EARNED INCOME-Income (especially wages and salaries) generated by providing goods or services. Also pension or annuity income.

ESTATE-All the assets a person possesses at the time of death-such as securities, real estate, interests in business, physical possessions, and cash.

EX-DIVIDEND-Interval between the announcement

A Funny Thing Happened on My Way to Work . . . I Retired

and the payment of the next dividend. An investor who buys shares during that interval is not entitled to the dividend. (See DATE OF RECORD).

F

FIFO-An accounting term meaning first in, first out.

FLAT MARKET-Market characterized by horizontal (sideways) price movement.

FRONT-END LOAD-Sales charge applied to an investment at the time of initial purchase. (Usually a Class A Mutual Fund).

FUND FAMILY-Mutual fund company offering funds with many investment objectives. (Conservative-Growth and Income-Growth-Aggressive).

G

GOING PUBLIC-Securities industry phrase used when a private company first offers its shares to the public.

GOOD-TILL-CANCELLED ORDER (GTC) Brokerage customer's order to buy or sell a security, usually at a particular price, that remains in effect until executed or cancelled.

GROSS DOMESTIC PRODUCT (GDP) Market value of the goods and services produced by labor and property *in* the United States.

GROWTH AND INCOME FUND-mutual fund that seeks earnings growth as well as income from dividend-paying stocks. (Conservative-**Growth and Income**-Growth-Aggressive).

GROWTH STOCK-Stock of a corporation that has exhibited faster-than-average gains in earnings over the last few years and is expected to continue to show high levels of profit growth. Stocks in this category usually pay little or no dividends.

H

HIGH-YIELD BOND-Bond that has a rating of BB or

lower and that pays a higher yield to compensate for its greater risk. (Also known as Junk Bonds).

I

INDIVIDUAL RETIREMENT ACCOUNT (IRA)-Personal, tax-deferred, retirement account that an employed person can set up. The individual must have earned income to qualify for an IRA contribution. Deductible amounts depend on the individuals AGI (Adjusted Gross Income).

INDIVIDUAL RETIREMENT ACCOUNT (IRA) ROLLOVER-Provision of the IRA law that enables persons receiving Lump-Sum payments from their company's defined contribution plan. A *direct transfer* made from one qualified plan such as a 401(k), to an IRA will roll over without any tax event. Only one rollover per year is allowed.

INITIAL PUBLIC OFFERING (IPO)-Corporation's first offering of stock to the public.

INSIDE INFORMATION-Corporate affairs that have not yet been made public. Under Securities and Exchange Commission rules, an INSIDER is not allowed to trade on the basis of such information.

INTEREST-ONLY LOAN-Increasingly popular loan for homeowners where the only current obligation is interest and where repayment of principal is deferred.

INVESTMENT GRADE-Bond with a rating of AAA to BBB.

INVESTMENT OBJECTIVE-Financial objective that an investor uses to determine which kind of investment is appropriate. This allows Advisors to recommend investments that are inline with the client's objective.

J

JOINT ACCOUNT-Brokerage account owned jointly by two or more people. (Example: JWROS-Joint With Rights Of Survivorship).

JOINT TENANTS WITH RIGHT OF SURVIVORSHIP-Is normally agreed that, upon death of one account holder, ownership of the account assets passes to the remaining account holder. This transfer of assets escapes probate, but estate taxes may be due.

JUNK BOND (see high-yield bond).

K

KNOW YOUR CUSTOMER-Ethical concept in the securities industry either stated or implied by the rules of the exchanges and other regulators. (Also known as rule 405).

L

LARGE CAP-Stock with a large capitalization (numbers of shares outstanding times the price of the shares). Large Cap stocks typically have at least $5 billion in outstanding MARKET VALUE.

LIFO-Accounting term for last in first out.

LIFE EXPECTANCY-Age to which an average person can be expected to live, as calculated by an ACTUARY. The IRS uses a life expectancy table to determine an individual's Required Minimum Distribution. (See RMD).

LIMIT ORDER-Order to buy or sell a security at a specific price *or better*.

LIQUID ASSET-Cash or easily convertible into cash. Example: Money Market funds, CDs, T-Bills).

LISTED SECURITY-Stock that has been accepted for trading by one of the organized and registered securities exchanges in the United States, which list more than 6000 issues of securities of some 3500 corporations. (Non-listed stocks are called Over The Counter or OTC).

LONG TERM

Holding period of 12 months or longer and applicable in calculating the CAPITAL GAINS TAX.

Bond with a maturity of 10 years or longer

M

MAINTENANCE CALL-Call for additional money or securities when a brokerage customer's margin account equity falls below the requirements of the National Association of Securities Dealers (NASD).

MANAGED ACCOUNT-Investment account consisting of money that one or more clients entrust to a manager, who decides when and where to invest it.

MARGIN-**In general:** amount a customer deposits with a broker when borrowing from the broker to buy securities.

MARGIN ACCOUNT-Brokerage account allowing customers to buy securities with money borrowed from the broker.

MARGIN CALL-Demand that a customer deposit enough money or securities to bring a margin account up to the INITIAL MARGIN requirements.

MARKET TIMING-Decisions on when to buy or sell securities based on various indicators.

MATURITY DATE-Date on which the principal amount of a note or bond becomes due and payable by the issuer.

MEDIUM-TERM BOND-Bond with a maturity of 2 to 10 years.

MID CAP-Stock with a middle-level capitalization (numbers of shares outstanding times the price of the shares). Mid Cap stocks typically have between $1 billion and $5 billion in outstanding market value.

MUNICIPAL BOND-Debt obligation of a state or local government entity that is backed by the entity's taxing power. Virtually all municipal obligations are exempt from federal income taxes and most from state and local income taxes, at least in the state of issue.

N

NASDAQ -National Association of Securities Dealers Automated Quotations system, which is owned and operated by the NASD.

A Funny Thing Happened on My Way to Work . . . I Retired

NATIONAL DEBT-Debt owed by the federal government.

NET ASSET VALUE (NAV)-In mutual funds, the market value of a fund share, synonymous with *bid price*.

NET WORTH-Amount by which assets exceed liabilities.

(Example: Assets–Liabilities = Net Worth).

NEW YORK STOCK EXCHANGE-Founded in 1792, it is the oldest and largest stock exchange in the U. S. located at 11 Wall Street in New York City; also known as the *Big Board* and *The Exchange*.

NONCALLABLE-Preferred stock or bond that cannot be redeemed at the option of the issuer.

O

ODD LOT-A securities trade made for less than the NORMAL TRADING UNIT (termed a ROUND LOT). A Round Lot consists of 100 shares.

OPEN ORDER-Status of an order to buy or sell securities that has still not been executed.

OPTION-**In general**: right to buy or sell property that is granted in exchange for an agreed upon sum. If the right is not exercised after a specified period, the option expires and the option buyer forfeits the money. (Common options are Calls and Puts).

OVER THE COUNTER (OTC)-Security that is not listed and traded on an organized exchange.

P

P & L-Profit and lost statement.

PAR-Equal to the nominal or face value of a security. For instance, a bond selling at par is worth the same dollar amount it was issued for-typically, $1000 per bond.

PENNY STOCK-Stock that typically sells for less than

$1 a share, and are generally very volatile. All penny stock are traded OVER-THE-COUNTER.

PIGGYBACKING-Illegal practice by a broker who buys or sells stocks or bonds in his personal account after a customer buys or sells the same security.

POWER OF ATTORNEY-**In general:** written document that authorizes a particular person to perform certain acts on behalf of the one signing the document.

PREFERRED STOCK-Class of CAPITAL STOCK that pays dividends at a specified rate and that has preference over common stock in the payment of dividends and the liquidation of assets.

PREMIUM BOND-Bond with a selling price above par value.

PRICE/EARNINGS RATIO (P/E)-Price of a stock divided by its earnings per share. The P/E ratio, also known as the *multiple,* gives investors an idea of how much they are paying for a company's earning power. The higher the P/E, the more "expensive" the stock.

PRIME RATE-Base rate that banks use in pricing commercial loans to their best and most creditworthy customers. The rate is determined by the Federal Reserve's decision to raise or lower prevailing interest rates for short-term borrowing.

PROBATE-Judicial process whereby the will of a deceased person is presented to a court and an EXECUTOR or ADMINISTRATOR is appointed to carry out the will's instructions. (Note: A will does *not* avoid probate, it guarantees it).

PROSPECTUS-Formal written offer to sell securities that sets forth the plan for a proposed business enterprise that an investor needs to make an informed decision.

Q

QUALIFIED MONEY-Money in a retirement plan, such as an IRA, that has never been taxed.

R

REAL ESTATE INVESTMENT TRUST (REIT)-Company, usually traded publicly, that manages a portfolio of real estate to earn profits for shareholders.

REAL RATE OF RETURN-Return on an investment adjusted for inflation.

RECESSION-Downturn in economic activity, defined by many economists as at least two consecutive quarters of decline in a country's GROSS DOMESTIC PRODUCT (GDP).

REVERSE SPLIT-Procedure whereby a corporation reduces the number of shares outstanding. (Example: You own 200 shares of XYZ stock worth $1000. After a 1 for 2 *reverse* split, you would own 100 shares of XYZ stock still worth $1000).

RMD-Required Minimum Distribution. The minimum amount that must be taken out of an individuals tax-deferred account (Such as an IRA) once he/she reaches 70 ½ . Failure to do so can result in an IRS penalty of 50% against the amount that should have been drawn out.

ROTH IRA-INDIVIDUAL RETIREMENT ACCOUNT created by the TAXPAYER RELIEF ACT OF 1997 permitting account holders to allow their capital to accumulate tax free under certain conditions. Roth contributions cannot be deducted from income whereas Traditional IRAs can-depending on AGI).

RULE OF 72-Formula for approximating the time it will take for a given amount of money to double at a given COMPOUND INTEREST rate. The formula is simply 72 divided by the interest rate. (Example: 8% compound interest rate. How long will it take your money to double at this rate? 72 divided by 8 = 9. At the rate of 8% it will take 9 years for your money to double).

S

SECONDARY MARKET-Exchanges and over-the-counter markets where securities are traded after their original issue, i.e. stocks, bonds, closed-end funds.

SELLING SHORT-Sale of a security not owned by the seller; a technique used to take advantage of an anticipated decline in the price. Keep in mind, the seller takes *unlimited* risk in a short sell. Theoretically, if the stock were to go up forever, so would the potential loss.

SETTLEMENT DATE-Date by which an executed order must be settled. In a REGULAR-WAY DELIVERY of stocks and bonds, the settlement is three business days after the trade was executed.

SPLIT-Increase in a corporation's number of outstanding shares of stock without any change in the shareholder's MARKET VALUE at the time of the split. Example: You own 100 shares of XYZ stock worth $1000. The stock splits 2 for 1; now you own 200 shares of XYZ stock worth $1000. (Exact opposite of a reverse split).

STANDARD & POOR'S 500 COMPOSITE INDEX-Broad-based measurement of changes in stock market conditions based on the average performance of 500 widely held common stocks, commonly known as the S & P 500.

T

TAXED DEFERRED-Term describing an investment whose accumulated earnings are free from taxation until the investor takes possession of them.

THIN MARKET-Market in which there are few bids to buy and few offers to sell. Generally, it is harder to unload (sell) a stock that is thinly traded since there are very few buyers.

TICKER SYMBOL-Letters that identify a security for trading purposes on the CONSOLIDATED TAPE. (Example: Wal-Mart, ticker symbol WMT).

U

UNEARNED INCOME-Income from sources other than

wages, salaries, tips, and other forms of employee compensation-for example: Dividends, Interest, Rent.

UNREALIZED PROFIT (OR LOSS)-Profit or loss that has not become actual. It becomes realized profit (or loss) when the security in which is a gain or loss is actually sold. (Example: If you purchased a security for $4000 and it is now worth $2000, but you still own the security, you have UNREALIZED LOSS. If, on the other hand, you decide to sell at the $2000 price, your losses become REALIZED or actual. The same is true of profits).

V

VOLATILITY-Characteristics of a security or market to rise or fall sharply in price within a short-term period.

W

WEAK DOLLAR-Dollar that has fallen in value against foreign currencies. This condition improves export trading since foreign money can buy more U. S. goods.

Y

YIELD TO CALL (ALSO KNOWN AS YIELD TO WORST)-Yield on a bond assuming the bond will be redeemed (called) by the issuer at the first call date instead of the bond reaching maturity.

YIELD TO MATURITY-Concept used to determine the rate of return an investor will receive if a long-term, interest-bearing investment, such as a bond, is held to its maturity date and never called.

Contact Steve Kiefer
or order more copies of this book at

TATE PUBLISHING, LLC

127 East Trade Center Terrace
Mustang, Oklahoma 73064

(888) 361 - 9473

Tate Publishing, LLC

www.tatepublishing.com